INTERNATIONAL ENCYCLOPEDIA *of* UNIFIED SCIENCE

Theory of Valuation

By

John Dewey

D1591187

VOLUMES I AND II · FOUNDATIONS OF THE UNITY OF SCIENCE

VOLUME II · NUMBER 4

International Encyclopedia of Unified Science

Editor-in-Chief Otto Neurath†

Associate Editors Rudolf Carnap Charles Morris

Foundations of the Unity of Science

(Volumes I–II of the Encyclopedia)

Committee of Organization

RUDOLF CARNAP   CHARLES W. MORRIS

PHILIPP FRANK†   OTTO NEURATH†

JOERGEN JOERGENSEN   LOUIS ROUGIER

†Deceased.

THE UNIVERSITY OF CHICAGO PRESS, CHICAGO 60637

The University of Chicago Press, Ltd., London

International Standard Book Number: 0–226–57594–2

Library of Congress Catalog Card Number: A42–5466

Contents:

Theory of Valuation

John Dewey

I. Its Problems

A skeptically inclined person viewing the present state of the discussion of valuing and values might find reason for concluding that a great ado is being made about very little, possibly about nothing at all. For the existing state of discussion shows not only that there is a great difference of opinion about the proper theoretical interpretation to be put upon facts, which might be a healthy sign of progress, but also that there is great disagreement as to what the facts are to which theory applies, and indeed whether there are any facts to which a theory of value can apply. For a survey of the current literature of the subject discloses that views on the subject range from the belief, at one extreme, that so-called "values" are but emotional epithets or mere ejaculations, to the belief, at the other extreme, that a priori necessary standardized, rational values are the principles upon which art, science, and morals depend for their validity. And between these two conceptions lies a number of intermediate views. The same survey will also disclose that discussion of the subject of "values" is profoundly affected by epistemological theories about idealism and realism and by metaphysical theories regarding the "subjective" and the "objective."

Given a situation of this sort, it is not easy to find a starting-point which is not compromised in advance. For what seems on the surface to be a proper starting-point may in fact be simply the conclusion of some prior epistemological or metaphysical theory. Perhaps it is safest to begin by asking how it is that the problem of valuation-theory has come to bulk so largely in recent discussions. Have there been any factors in intellectual history which have produced such marked changes in scientific attitudes and conceptions as to throw the problem into relief?

When one looks at the problem of valuation in this context, one is at once struck by the fact that the sciences of astronomy, physics, chemistry, etc., do not contain expressions that by any stretch of the imagination can be regarded as standing for value-facts or conceptions. But, on the other hand, all deliberate, all planned human conduct, personal and collective, seems to be influenced, if not controlled, by estimates of value or worth of ends to be attained. Good sense in practical affairs is generally identified with a sense of relative values. This contrast between natural science and human affairs apparently results in a bifurcation, amounting to a radical split. There seems to be no ground common to the conceptions and methods that are taken for granted in all physical matters and those that appear to be most important in respect to human activities. Since the propositions of the natural sciences concern matters-of-fact and the relations between them, and since such propositions constitute the subject matter acknowledged to possess pre-eminent scientific standing, the question inevitably arises whether scientific propositions about the direction of human conduct, about any situation into which the idea of *should* enters, are possible; and, if so, of what sort they are and the grounds upon which they rest.

The elimination of value-conceptions from the science of nonhuman phenomena is, from a historical point of view, comparatively recent. For centuries, until, say, the sixteenth and seventeenth centuries, nature was supposed to be what it is because of the presence within it of *ends*. In their very capacity as ends they represented complete or *perfect* Being. All natural changes were believed to be striving to actualize these ends as the goals toward which they moved by their own nature. Classic philosophy identified *ens*, *verum*, and *bonum*, and the identification was taken to be an expression of the constitution of nature as the object of natural science. In such a context there was no call and no place for any *separate* problem of valuation and values, since what are now termed values were taken to be integrally incorporated in the very structure of the world. But when teleological considerations were eliminated from one natural science after another, and finally from the sciences of physiology and biology, the problem of value arose as a separate problem.

If it is asked why it happened that, with the exclusion from nature of conceptions of ends and of striving to attain them, the conception of values did not entirely drop out—as did, for example, that of phlogiston—the answer is suggested by what has been said about the place of conceptions and estimates of value in distinctively human affairs. Human behavior *seems* to be influenced, if not controlled, by considerations such as are expressed in the words 'good-bad,' 'right-wrong,' 'admirable-hideous,' etc. All conduct that is not simply either blindly impulsive or mechanically routine seems to involve valuations. The problem of valuation is thus closely associated with the problem of the structure of the sciences of *human* activities and *human* relations. When the problem of valuation is placed in this context, it begins to be clear that the problem is one of moment. The various and conflicting theories that are entertained about valuation also take on significance. For those who hold that the field of scientifically warranted propositions is exhausted in the field of propositions of physics and chemistry will be led to hold that there are no genuine value-propositions or judgments, no propositions that state (affirm or **deny**) anything about values capable of support and test by experimental evidence. Others, who accept the distinction between the nonpersonal field and the personal or human field as one of two separate fields of existence, the physical and the mental or psychical, will hold that the elimination of value-categories from the physical field makes it clear that they are located in the mental. A third school employs the fact that value-expressions are not found in the physical sciences as proof that the subject matter of the physical sciences is only partial (sometimes called merely "phenomenal") and hence needs to be supplemented by a "higher" type of subject matter and knowledge in which value-categories are supreme over those of factual existence.

The views just listed are typical but not exhaustive. They are listed not so much to indicate the theme of discussion as to help delimit the central problem about which discussions turn, often, apparently, without being aware of their source; namely, the problem of the possibility of genuine propositions about the direction of human affairs. Were it possible, it would probably be desirable to discuss this problem with a minimum of explicit reference to value-expressions. For much ambiguity has been imported into discussion of the latter from outside epistemological and psychological sources. Since this mode of approach is not possible under existing circumstances, this introductory section will conclude with some remarks about certain linguistic expressions purporting to designate distinctive value-facts.

1. The expression 'value' is used as a verb and a noun, and there is a basic dispute as to which sense is primary. If there are things that are values or that have the property of value apart from connection with any activity, then the verb 'to value' is derivative. For in this case an act of apprehension is called valuation simply because of the object it grasps. If, however, the active sense, designated by a verb, is primary, then the noun 'value' designates what common speech calls a *valuable*—something that is the object of a certain kind of activity. For example, things which exist independently of being valued, like diamonds or mines and forests, are valuable when they are the objects of certain human activities. There are many nouns designating things not in their primary existence but as the material or objectives (as when something is called a target) of activities. The question whether this holds in the case of a thing (or the property) called value is one of the matters involved in controversy. Take, for example, the following quotations. Value is said to be "best defined as the qualitative content of an apprehending process. . . . . It is a given qualitative content present to attention or intuition." This statement would seem to take 'value' as primarily a noun, or at least an adjective, designating an object or its intrinsic quality. But when the same author goes on to speak of the process of intuiting and apprehending, he says: "What seems to distinguish

the act of valuing from the bare act of intuiting is that the former is qualified, to a noticeable degree, by feeling. . . . . It consciously discriminates some specific content. But the act of valuing is also emotional; it is the conscious expression of an interest, a motor-affective attitude." This passage gives the opposite impression of the one previously cited. Nor is the matter made clearer when it is further said that "the value-quality or content of the experience has been distinguished from the value-act or psychological attitude of which this content is the immediate object"—a position that seems like an attempt to solve a problem by riding two horses going in opposite directions.

Furthermore, when attention is confined to the usage of the verb 'to value,' we find that common speech exhibits a double usage. For a glance at the dictionary will show that in ordinary speech the words 'valuing' and 'valuation' are verbally employed to designate both *prizing*, in the sense of holding precious, dear (and various other nearly equivalent activities, like honoring, regarding highly), and *appraising* in the sense of *putting* a value upon, *assigning* value to. This is an activity of rating, an act that involves comparison, as is explicit, for example, in appraisals in money terms of goods and services. The double meaning is significant because there is implicit in it one of the basic issues regarding valuation. For in *prizing*, emphasis falls upon something having definite *personal* reference, which, like all activities of distinctively personal reference, has an aspectual quality called emotional. Valuation as *appraisal*, however, is primarily concerned with a relational property of objects so that an intellectual aspect is uppermost of the same general sort that is found in '*estimate*' as distinguished from the personal-emotional word '*esteem*.' That the same verb is employed in both senses suggests the problem upon which schools are divided at the present time. Which of the two references is basic in its implications? Are the two activities separate or are they complementary? In connection with etymological history, it is suggestive (though, of course, in no way conclusive) that 'praise,' 'prize,' and 'price' are all derived from the same Latin word; that 'appreciate' and 'appraise' were once used interchangeably; and that 'dear' is still used as equivalent both to 'precious' and to 'costly' in monetary price. While the dual significance of the word as used in ordinary speech raises a problem, the question of linguistic usage is further extended—not to say confused—by the fact that current theories often identify the verb 'to value' with 'to enjoy' in the sense of receiving pleasure or gratification from something, finding it agreeable; and also with 'to enjoy' in the active sense of *concurring* in an activity and its outcome.

2. If we take certain words commonly regarded as value-expressions, we find no agreement in theoretical discussions as to their proper status. There are, for example, those who hold that 'good' means *good for*, useful, serviceable, helpful; while 'bad' means harmful, detrimental—a conception which contains implicitly a complete theory of valuation. Others hold that a sharp difference exists between good in the sense of 'good for' and that which is 'good in itself.' Again, as just noted, there are those who hold that 'pleasant' and 'gratifying' are value-expressions of the first rank, while others would not give them standing as primary value-expressions. There is also dispute as to the respective status of 'good' and 'right' as value-words.

The conclusion is that verbal usage gives us little help. Indeed, when it is used to give direction to the discussion, it proves confusing. The most that reference to linguistic expressions can do at the outset is to point out certain problems. These problems may be used to delimit the topic under discussion. As far, then, as the terminology of the present discussion is concerned, the word 'valuation' will be used, both verbally and as a noun, as the most neutral in its theoretical implications, leaving it to further discussion to determine its connection with *prizing, appraising, enjoying,* etc.

II. Value-Expression as Ejaculatory

Discussion will begin with consideration of the most extreme of the views which have been advanced. This view affirms that value-expressions cannot be constituents of propositions, that is, of sentences which affirm or deny, because they are purely ejaculatory. Such expressions as 'good,' 'bad,' 'right,' 'wrong,' 'lovely,' 'hideous,' etc., are regarded as of the same nature as interjections; or as phenomena like blushing, smiling, weeping; or/and as stimuli to move others to act in certain ways—much as one says "Gee" to oxen or "Whoa" to a horse. They do not say or state anything, not even about feelings; they merely evince or manifest the latter.

The following quotations represent this view: "If I say to some one, 'You acted wrongly in stealing that money,' I am not *stating* anything more than if I had simply said 'You stole that money.' . . . . It is as if I had said 'You stole that money' in a peculiar tone of horror, or written it with the addition of some special exclamation marks. The tone . . . . merely serves to show that the expression is attended by certain feelings in the speaker." And again: "Ethical terms do not serve only to express feelings. They are calculated also to arouse feeling and so to stimulate action. . . . . Thus the sentence 'It is your duty to tell the truth' may be regarded both as the expression of a certain sort of ethical feeling about truthfulness and as the expression of the command 'Tell the truth.' . . . . In the sentence 'It is good to tell the truth' the command has become little more than a suggestion." On what grounds the writer calls the terms and the "feelings" of which he speaks "ethical" does not appear. Nevertheless, applying this adjective to the feelings seems to involve some objective ground for discriminating and identifying them as of a certain kind, a conclusion inconsistent with the position taken. But, ignoring this fact, we pass on to a further illustration: "In saying 'tolerance is a virtue' I should not be making a statement about my own feelings or about anything else. I should simply be evincing my own feelings, which is not at all the same thing as saying that I have them." Hence "it is impossible to dispute about questions of value," for sentences that do not say or state anything whatever cannot, a fortiori, be incompatible with one another. Cases of apparent dispute or of opposed statements are, if they have any meaning

at all, reducible to differences regarding the facts of the case—
as there might be a dispute whether a man performed the particular action called stealing or lying. Our hope or expectation
is that if "we can get an opponent to agree with us about the
empirical facts of the case he will adopt the same moral attitude
toward them as we do"—though once more it is not evident
why the attitude is called "moral" rather than "magical,"
"belligerent," or any one of thousands of adjectives that might
be selected at random.

Discussion will proceed, as has previously been intimated, by
analyzing the facts that are appealed to and not by discussing
the merits of the theory in the abstract. Let us begin with
phenomena that admittedly say nothing, like the first cries of a
baby, his first smiles, or his early cooings, gurglings, and squeals.
When it is said that they "express feelings," there is a danger-
ous ambiguity in the words 'feelings' and 'express.' What is
clear in the case of tears or smiles ought to be clear in the case
of sounds involuntarily uttered. They are not in themselves
expressive. They are constituents of a larger organic condition.
They are facts of organic behavior and are *not* in any sense
whatever value-expressions. They may, however, be taken by
other persons as *signs* of an organic state, and, so taken, *qua*
signs or treated as *symptoms*, they evoke certain responsive
forms of behavior in these other persons. A baby cries. The
mother takes the cry as a sign the baby is hungry or that a pin
is pricking it, and so acts to change the organic condition in-
ferred to exist by using the cry as an evidential sign.

Then, as the baby matures, it becomes aware of the connection that exists between a certain cry, the activity evoked, and
the consequences produced in response to it. The cry (gesture,
posture) is now made *in order* to evoke the activity and in order
to experience the consequences of that activity. Just as with
respect to the original response there is a difference between the
activity that is merely *caused* by the cry as a stimulus (as the
cry of a child may awaken a sleeping mother before she is even
aware there is a cry) and an activity that is evoked by the cry
interpreted as a *sign* or evidence of something, so there is a dif-

ference between the original cry—which may properly be called purely ejaculatory—and the cry made on purpose, that is, with the intent to evoke a response that will have certain consequences. The latter cry exists in the medium of language; it is a linguistic sign that not only says something but is intended to say, to convey, to tell.

What is it which is then told or stated? In connection with this question, a fatal ambiguity in the word 'feelings' requires notice. For perhaps the view will be propounded that at most all that is communicated is the existence of certain feelings along perhaps with a desire to obtain other feelings in consequence of the activity evoked in another person. But any such view (*a*) goes contrary to the obvious facts with which the account began and (*b*) introduces a totally superfluous not to say empirically unverifiable matter. (*a*) For what we started with was not a feeling but an organic condition of which a cry, or tears, or a smile, or a blush, is a constituent part. (*b*) The word 'feelings' is accordingly either a strictly behavioral term, a name for the total organic state of which the cry or gesture is a part, or it is a word which is introduced entirely gratuitously. The phenomena in question are events in the course of the life of an organic being, not differing from taking food or gaining weight. But just as a gain in weight may be taken as a sign or evidence of proper feeding, so the cry may be taken as a sign or evidence of some special occurrence in organic life.

The phrase 'evincing feeling,' whether or not 'evincing' is taken as a synonym of 'expressing,' has, then, no business in the report of what takes place. The original activity—crying, smiling, weeping, squealing—is, as we have seen, a part of a larger organic state, so the phrase does not apply to it. When the cry or bodily attitude is purposely made, it is not a feeling that is evinced or expressed. Overt linguistic behavior is undertaken so as to obtain a change in organic conditions—a change to occur as the result of some behavior undertaken by some other person. Take another simple example: A smacking of the lips is or may be part of the original behavioral action called taking food. In one social group the noise made in smacking the lips is treated as a sign of boorishness or of "bad manners." Hence as the young grow in power of muscular control, they are taught to inhibit this activity. In another social group smacking the lips and the accompanying noise are taken as a sign that a guest is properly aware of what the host has provided. Both cases are completely describable in terms of observable modes of behavior and their respective observable consequences.

The serious problem in this connection is why the word 'feelings' is introduced in the theoretical account, since it is unnecessary in report of what actually happens. There is but one reasonable answer. The word is brought in from an alleged psychological theory which is couched in mentalistic terms, or in terms of alleged states of an inner consciousness or something of that sort. Now it is irrelevant and unnecessary to ask in connection with events before us whether there are in fact such inner states. For, even if there be such states, they are by description wholly private, accessible only to private inspection. Consequently, even if there were a legitimate introspectionist theory of states of consciousness or of feelings as purely mentalistic, there is no justification for borrowing from this theory in giving an account of the occurrences under examination. The reference to "feelings" is superfluous and gratuitous, moreover, because the important part of the account given is the use of "value-expressions" to influence the conduct of others by evoking certain responses from them. From the standpoint of an empirical report it is meaningless, since the interpretation is couched in terms of something not open to public inspection and verification. If there are "feelings" of the kind mentioned, there cannot be any assurance that any given word when used by two different persons even refers to the same thing, since the thing is not open to common observation and description.

Confining further consideration, then, to the part of the account that has an empirical meaning, namely, the existence of organic activities which evoke certain responses from others and which are capable of being employed with a view to evoking them, the following statements are warranted: (1) The phenomena in question are *social* phenomena where 'social' means simply that there is a form of behavior of the nature of an interaction or transaction between two or more persons. Such an interpersonal activity exists whenever one person— as a mother or nurse—treats a sound made by another person incidentally to a more extensive organic behavior *as a sign*, and responds to it in that capacity instead of reacting to it in its primary existence. The interpersonal activity is even more evident when the item of organic personal behavior in question takes place *for the sake of* evoking a certain kind of response from other persons. If, then, we follow the writer in locating value-expressions where he located them, we are led, after carrying out the required elimination of the ambiguity of 'expression' and the irrelevance of 'feeling,' to the conclusions that value-expressions have to do with or are involved in the behavioral relations of persons to one another. (2) Taken as signs (and, a fortiori, when used as signs) gestures, postures, and words are linguistic symbols. They say something and are of the nature of propositions. Take, for example, the case of a person who assumes the posture appropriate to an ailing person and who utters sounds such as the latter person would ordinarily make. It is then a legitimate subject of inquiry whether the person is genuinely ailing and incapacitated for work or is malingering. The conclusions obtained as a result of the inquiries undertaken will certainly "evoke" from other persons very different kinds of responsive behavior. The investigation is carried on to determine what is the actual case of things that are empirically observable; it is not about inner "feelings." Physicians have worked out experimental tests that have a high degree of reliability. Every parent and schoolteacher learns to be on guard against the assuming by a child of certain facial "expressions" and bodily attitudes for the purpose of causing inferences to be drawn which are the source of favor on the part of the adult. In such cases (they could easily be extended to include more complex matters) the propositions that embody the inference are likely to be in error when only a short segment of behavior is observed and are likely to be warranted when they rest upon a prolonged segment or upon a variety of carefully scrutinized data—traits that the propositions in question have in common with all genuine physical propositions. (3) So far the question has not been raised as to whether the propositions that occur in the course of interpersonal behavioral situations are or are not of the nature of valuation-propositions. The conclusions reached are hypothetical. *If* the expressions involved are valuation-expressions, as this particular school takes them to be, *then* it follows (i) that valuation-phenomena are social or interpersonal phenomena and (ii) that they are such as to provide material for propositions about observable events—propositions subject to empirical test and verification or refutation. But so far the hypothesis remains a hypothesis. It raises the question whether the statements which occur with a view to influencing the activity of others, so as to call out from them certain modes of activity having certain consequences, are phenomena falling under the head of valuation.

Take, for example, the case of a person calling "Fire!" or "Help!" There can be no doubt of the intent to influence the conduct of others in order to bring about certain consequences capable of observation and of statement in propositions. The expressions, taken in their observable context, say something of a complex character. When analyzed, what is said is (i) that there exists a situation that will have obnoxious consequences; (ii) that the person uttering the expressions is unable to cope with the situation; and (iii) that an improved situation is anticipated in case the assistance of others is obtained. All three of these matters are capable of being tested by empirical evidence, since they all refer to things that are observable. The proposition in which the content of the last point (the anticipation) is stated is capable, for example, of being tested by observation of what happens in a particular case. Previous observations may substantiate the conclusion that in any case objectionable consequences are much less likely to happen if the linguistic sign is employed in order to obtain the assistance it is designed to evoke.

Examination shows certain resemblances between these cases and those previously examined which, according to the passage quoted, contain valuation-expressions. The propositions refer directly to an *existing* situation and indirectly to a *future* situation which it is intended and desired to produce. The expressions noted are employed as intermediaries to bring about the desired change from present to future conditions. In the set of illustrative cases that was first examined, certain valuation-words, like 'good' and 'right,' explicitly appear; in the second set there are no *explicit* value-expressions. The cry for aid, however, when taken in connection with its existential context, affirms in effect, although not in so many words, that the situation with reference to which the cry is made is "bad." It is "bad" in the sense that it is objected to, while a future situation which is *better* is anticipated, provided the cry evokes a certain response. The analysis may seem to be unnecessarily detailed. But, unless in each set of examples the existential context is made clear, the verbal expressions that are employed can be made to mean anything or nothing. When the contexts are taken into account, what emerges are propositions assigning a relatively negative value to existing conditions; a comparatively positive value to a prospective set of conditions; and intermediate propositions (which may or may not contain a valuation-expression) intended to evoke activities that will bring about a transformation from one state of affairs to another. There are thus involved (i) aversion to an existing situation and attraction toward a prospective possible situation and (ii) a *specifiable and testable relation between the latter as an end and certain activities as means for accomplishing it.* Two problems for further discussion are thus set. One of them is the relation of active or behavioral attitudes to what may be called (for the purpose of identification) *liking* and *disliking*, while the other is the relation of valuation to things as means-end.

III. Valuation as Liking and Disliking

That liking and disliking in their connection with valuation are to be considered in terms of observable and identifiable modes of behavior follows from what is stated in the previous section. As behavioral the adjective 'affective-motor' is applicable, although care must be taken not to permit the "affective" quality to be interpreted in terms of private "feelings"—an interpretation that nullifies the active and observable element expressed in 'motor.' For the "motor" takes place in the public and observable world, and, like anything else taking place there, has observable conditions and consequences. When, then, the word 'liking' is used as a name for a mode of behavior (not as a name for a private and inaccessible feeling), what sort of activities does it stand for? What is its designatum? This inquiry is forwarded by noting that the words 'caring' and 'caring for' are, as modes of behavior, closely connected with 'liking,' and that other substantially equivalent words are 'looking out for or after,' 'cherishing,' 'being devoted to,' 'attending to,' in the sense of 'tending', 'ministering to,' 'fostering'— words that all seem to be variants of what is referred to by 'prizing,' which, as we saw earlier, is one of the two main significations recognized by the dictionary. When these words are taken in the behavioral sense, or as naming activities that take place so as to maintain or procure certain conditions, it is possible to demarcate what is designated by them from things designated by such an ambiguous word as 'enjoy.' For the latter word may point to a condition of *receiving* gratification *from* something already in existence, apart from any affective-motor action exerted as a condition of its production or continued existence. Or it may refer to precisely the latter activity, in which case 'to enjoy' is a synonym for the activity of taking delight in an effort, having a certain overtone of relishing, which "takes pains," as we say, to perpetuate *the existence of conditions* from which gratification is received. Enjoying in this active sense is marked by energy expended to secure the conditions that are the source of the gratification.

The foregoing remarks serve the purpose of getting theory away from a futile task of trying to assign signification to words in isolation from objects as designata. We are led instead to evocation of specifiable existential situations and to observation of what takes place in them. We are directed to observe whether energy is put forth to call into existence or to maintain in existence certain conditions; in ordinary language, to note whether effort is evoked, whether pains are taken to bring about the existence of certain conditions rather than others, the need for expenditure of energy showing that there exist conditions adverse to what is wanted. The mother who professes to prize her child and to enjoy (in the active sense of the word) the child's companionship but who systematically neglects the child and does not seek out occasions for being with the child is deceiving herself; if she makes, in addition, demonstrative signs of affection—like fondling—only when others are present, she is presumably trying to deceive them also. It is by observations of behavior—which observations (as the last illustration suggests) may need to be extended over a considerable space-time —that the existence and description of valuations have to be determined. Observation of the amount of energy expended and the length of time over which it persists enables qualifying adjectives like 'slight' and 'great' to be warrantably prefixed to a given valuation. The direction the energy is observed to take, as toward and away from, enables grounded discrimination to be made between "positive" and "negative" valuations. If there are "feelings" existing in addition, their existence has nothing to do with any verifiable proposition that can be made about a valuation.

Because valuations in the sense of prizing and caring for occur only when it is necessary to bring something into existence which is lacking, or to conserve in existence something which is menaced by outside conditions, valuation *involves* desiring. The latter is to be distinguished from mere wishing in the sense in which wishes occur in the absence of effort. "If wishes were horses, beggars would ride." There is something lacking, and it would be gratifying if it were present, but there is either no energy expended to bring what is absent into existence or else, under the given conditions, no expenditure of effort would bring it into existence—as when the baby is said to cry for the moon, and when infantile adults indulge in dreams about how nice everything would be if things were only different. The *designata* in the cases to which the names 'desiring' and 'wishing' are respectively applied are basically different. When, accordingly, 'valuation' is defined in terms of desiring, the prerequisite is a treatment of desire in terms of the existential context in which it arises and functions. If 'valuation' is defined in terms of desire as something initial and complete in itself, there is nothing by which to discriminate one desire from another and hence no way in which to measure the worth of different valuations in comparison with one another. Desires are desires, and that is all that can be said. Furthermore, desire is then conceived of as *merely* personal and hence as not capable of being stated in terms of other objects or events. If, for example, it should happen to be noted that effort ensues upon desire and that the effort put forth changes existing conditions, these considerations would then be looked upon as matters wholly external to desire—provided, that is, desire is taken to be original and complete in itself, independent of an observable contextual situation.

When, however, desires are seen to arise only within certain existential contexts (namely, those in which some lack prevents the immediate execution of an active tendency) and when they are seen to function in reference to these contexts in such a way as to make good the existing want, the relation between desire and *valuation* is found to be such as both to make possible, and to require, statement in verifiable propositions. (i) The content and object of desires are seen to depend upon the particular context in which they arise, a matter that in turn depends upon the antecedent state of both personal activity and of surrounding conditions. Desires for food, for example, will hardly be the same if one has eaten five hours or five days previously, nor will they be of the same content in a hovel and a palace or in a nomadic or agricultural group. (ii) Effort, instead of being something that comes after desire, is seen to be of the very essence of the tension involved in desire. For the latter, instead of being merely personal, is an active relation of the organism to the environment (as is obvious in the case of hunger), a factor that makes the difference between genuine desire and mere wish and fantasy. It follows that valuation in its connection with desire is linked to existential situations and that it differs with differences in its existential context. Since its existence depends upon the situation, its adequacy depends upon its adaptation to the needs and demands imposed by the situation. Since the situation is open to observation, and since the consequences of effort-behavior as observed determine the adaptation, the adequacy of a given desire can be stated in propositions. The propositions are capable of empirical test because the connection that exists between a given desire and the conditions with reference to which it functions are ascertained by means of these observations.

The word 'interest' suggests in a forcible way the active connection between personal activity and the conditions that must be taken into account in the theory of valuation. Even in etymology it indicates something in which both a person and surrounding conditions participate in intimate connection with one another. In naming this something that occurs between them it names a transaction. It points to an activity which takes effect through the mediation of external conditions. When we think, for example, of the interest of any particular group, say the bankers' interest, the trade-union interest, or the interest of a political machine, we think not of mere states of mind but of the group as a pressure group having organized channels in which it directs action to obtain and make secure conditions that will produce specified consequences. Similarly in the case of singular persons, when a court recognizes an individual as having an interest in some matter, it recognizes that he has certain claims whose enforcement will affect an existential issue or outcome. Whenever a person has an interest in something, he has a stake in the course of events and in their final issue—a stake which leads him to take action to bring into existence a particular result rather than some other one.

It follows from the facts here adduced that the view which connects valuation (and "values") with desires and interest is but a starting-point. It is indeterminate in its bearing upon the theory of valuation until the nature of interest and desire has been analyzed, and until a method has been established for determining the constituents of desires and interests in their concrete particular occurrence. Practically all the fallacies in the theories that connect valuation with desire result from taking "desire" at large. For example, when it is said (quite correctly) that "values *spring from* the immediate and inexplicable reaction of vital impulse and from the irrational part of our nature," what is actually stated is that vital impulses are a *causal condition* of the existence of desires. When "vital impulse" is given the only interpretation which is empirically verifiable (that of an organic biological tendency), the fact that an "irrational" factor is the causal condition of valuations proves that valuations have their roots *in an existence* which, like any existence *taken in itself*, is *a*-rational. Correctly interpreted, the statement is thus a reminder that organic tendencies are existences which are connected with other existences (the word 'irrational' adds nothing to "*existence*" as such) and hence are observable. But the sentence cited is often interpreted to mean that vital impulses *are* valuations—an interpretation which is incompatible with the view which connects valuations with desires and interests, and which, by parity of logic, would justify the statement that trees are seeds since they "spring from" seeds. Vital impulses are doubtless conditions *sine qua non* for the existence of desires and interests. But the latter include foreseen consequences along with ideas in the form of signs of the measures (involving expenditure of energy) required to bring the ends into existence. When valuation is identified with the activity of desire or interest, its identification with vital impulse is denied. For its identification with the latter would lead to the absurdity of making every organic activity of every kind an act of valuation, since there is none that does not involve some "vital impulse."

The view that "a value is any object of any interest" must also be taken with great caution. On its face it places all interests on exactly the same level. But, when interests are examined in their concrete makeup in relation to their place in some situation, it is plain that everything depends upon the objects involved in them. This in turn depends upon the care with which the needs of existing situations have been looked into and upon the care with which the ability of a proposed act to satisfy or fulfil just those needs has been examined. That all interests stand on the same footing with respect to their function as valuators is contradicted by observation of even the most ordinary of everyday experiences. It may be said that an interest in burglary and its fruits confers value upon certain objects. But the valuations of the burglar and the policeman are not identical, any more than the interest in the fruits of productive work institutes the same values as does the interest of the burglar in the pursuit of his calling—as is evident in the action of a judge when stolen goods are brought before him for disposition. Since interests occur in definite existential contexts and not at large in a void, and since these contexts are situations within the life-activity of a person or group, interests are so linked with one another that the valuation-capacity of any one is a function of the set to which it belongs. The notion that a value is equally any object of any interest can be maintained only upon a view that completely isolates them from one another—a view that is so removed from readily observed facts that its existence can be explained only as a corollary of the introspectionist psychology which holds that desires and interests are but "feelings" instead of modes of behavior.

IV. Propositions of Appraisal

Since desires and interests are activities which take place in the world and which have effects in the world, they are observable in themselves and in connection with their observed effects. It might seem then as if, upon any theory that relates valuation with desire and interest, we had now come within sight of our goal—the discovery of valuation-propositions. Propositions *about* valuations have, indeed, been shown to be possible. But they are valuation-propositions only in the sense in which propositions about potatoes are potato-propositions. They are propositions about matters-of-fact. The fact that these occurrences happen to be valuations does not make the propositions valuation-propositions in any distinctive sense. Nevertheless, the fact that such matter-of-fact propositions can be made is of importance. For, unless they exist, it is doubly absurd to suppose that valuation-propositions in a *distinctive* sense can exist. It has also been shown that the subject matter of personal activities forms no theoretical barrier to institution of matter-of-fact propositions, for the behavior of human beings is open to observation. While there are practical obstacles to the establishment of valid general propositions about such behavior (i.e., about the relations of its constituent acts), its conditions and effects may be investigated. Propositions about valuations made in terms of their conditions and consequences delimit the problem as to existence of valuation-propositions in a *distinctive* sense. Are propositions about existent valuations themselves capable of being appraised, and can the appraisal when made enter into the constitution of further valuations? That a mother prizes or holds dear her child, we have seen, may be determined by observation; and the conditions and effects of different kinds of prizing or caring for may, in theory, be compared and contrasted with one another. In case the final outcome is to show that some kinds of acts of prizing are *better* than others, valuation-acts are themselves evaluated, and the evaluation may modify further direct acts of prizing. If this condition is satisfied, then propositions about valuations that actually take place become the subject matter of valuations in a distinctive sense, that is, a sense that marks them off both from propositions of physics and from historical propositions about what human beings have in fact done.

We are brought thus to the problem of the nature of appraisal or evaluation which, as we saw, is one of the two recognized significations of 'valuation.' Take such an elementary appraisal proposition as "This plot of ground is worth $200 a front foot." It is different in form from the proposition, "It has a frontage of 200 feet." The latter sentence states a matter of accomplished fact. The former sentence states a rule for determination of an act to be performed, its reference being to the future and not to something already accomplished or done. If stated in the context in which a tax-assessor operates, it states a regulative condition for levying a tax against the owner; if stated by the owner to a real estate dealer, it sets forth a regulative condition to be observed by the latter in offering the property for sale. The future act or state is not set forth as a prediction of what will happen but as something which *shall* or *should* happen. Thus the proposition may be said to lay down a norm, but "norm" must be understood simply in the sense of a condition *to be* conformed to in definite forms of future action. That rules are all but omnipresent in every mode of human relationship is too obvious to require argument. They are in no way confined to activities to which the name 'moral' is applied. Every recurrent form of activity, in the arts and professions, develops rules as to the best way in which to accomplish the ends in view. Such rules are used as criteria or "norms" for judging the value of proposed modes of behavior. The existence of rules for valuation of modes of behavior in different fields as wise or unwise, economical or extravagant, effective or futile, cannot be denied. The problem concerns not their existence as general propositions (since every rule of action is general) but whether they express only custom, convention, tradition, or are capable of stating relations between things as means and other things as consequences, which relations are themselves grounded in empirically ascertained and tested existential relations such as are usually termed those of cause and effect.

In the case of some crafts, arts, and technologies, there can be no doubt which of these alternatives is correct. The medical art, for example, is approaching a state in which many of the rules laid down for a patient by a physician as to what it is *better* for him to do, not merely in the way of medicaments but of diet and habits of life, are based upon experimentally ascertained principles of chemistry and physics. When engineers say that certain materials subjected to certain technical operations are *required* if a bridge capable of supporting certain loads is to be built over the Hudson River at a certain point, their advice does not represent their personal opinions or whims but is backed by acknowledged physical laws. It is commonly believed that such devices as radios and automobiles have been greatly improved (bettered) since they were first invented, and that the betterment in the relation of means to consequences is due to more adequate scientific knowledge of underlying physical principles. The argument does not demand the belief that the influence of custom and convention is entirely eliminated. It is enough that such cases show that it is possible for rules of appraisal or evaluation to rest upon scientifically warranted physical generalizations and that the ratio of rules of this type to those expressing mere customary habits is on the increase.

In medicine a quack may cite a number of alleged cures as evidential ground for taking the remedies he offers. Only a little examination is needed to show in what definite respects the procedures he recommends differ from those said to be "good" or to be "required" by competent physicians. There is, for example, no analysis of the cases presented as evidence to show that they are actually like the disease for the cure of which the remedy is urged; and there is no analysis to show that the recoveries which are said (rather than proved) to have taken place were in fact due to taking the medicine in question rather than to any one of an indefinite number of other causes. Everything is asserted wholesale with no analytic control of conditions. Furthermore, the first requirement of scientific procedure— namely, full publicity as to materials and processes—is lacking. The sole justification for citing these familiar facts is that their contrast with competent medical practice shows the extent to which the rules of procedure in the latter art have the warrant of tested empirical propositions. Appraisals of courses of action as better and worse, more and less serviceable, are as experimentally justified as are nonvaluative propositions about impersonal subject matter. In advanced engineering technologies propositions that state the *proper* courses of action to be adopted are evidently grounded in generalizations of physical and chemical science; they are often referred to as *applied* science. Nevertheless, propositions which lay down rules for procedures as being fit and good, as distinct from those that are inept and bad, are different in form from the scientific propositions upon which they rest. For they are rules for the use, in and by human activity, of scientific generalizations as means for accomplishing certain desired and intended ends.

Examination of these appraisals discloses that they have to do with things as they sustain to each other the relation of *means to ends or consequences.* Wherever there is an appraisal involving a rule as to better or as to needed action, there is an end to be reached: the appraisal is a valuation of things with respect to their serviceability or needfulness. If we take the examples given earlier, it is evident that real estate is appraised for the purpose of levying taxes or fixing a selling price; that medicinal treatments are appraised with reference to the end of effecting recovery of health; that materials and techniques are valued with respect to the building of bridges, radios, motorcars, etc. If a bird builds its nest by what is called pure "instinct," it does not have to appraise materials and processes with respect to their fitness for an end. But if the result—the nest—is contemplated as an object of desire, then either there is the most arbitrary kind of trial-and-error operations or there is consideration of the fitness and usefulness of materials and processes to bring the desired object into existence. And this process of weighing obviously involves comparison of different materials and operations as alternative possible means. In every case, except those of sheer "instinct" and complete trial and error, there are involved observation of actual materials and estimate of their potential force in production of a particular result. There is always some observation of the *outcome attained* in comparison and contrast with that intended, such that the comparison throws light upon the actual fitness of the things employed as means. It thus makes possible a better judgment in the future as to their fitness and usefulness. On the basis of such observations certain modes of conduct are adjudged silly, imprudent, or unwise, and other modes of conduct sensible, prudent, or wise, the discrimination being made upon the basis of the validity of the estimates reached about the relation of things as means to the end or consequence actually reached.

The standing objection raised against this view of valuation is that it applies only to things *as means*, while propositions that are genuine valuations apply to things as *ends*. This point will be shortly considered at length. But it may be noted here that ends are appraised in the same evaluations in which things as means are weighed. For example, an end suggests itself. But, when things are weighed as means toward that end, it is found that it will take too much time or too great an expenditure of energy to achieve it, or that, if it were attained, it would bring with it certain accompanying inconveniences and the promise of future troubles. It is then appraised and rejected as a "bad" end.

The conclusions reached may be summarized as follows: (1) There are propositions which are not merely about valuations that have actually occurred (about, i.e., prizings, desires, and interests that have taken place in the past) but which describe and define certain things as good, fit, or proper in a definite existential relation: these propositions, moreover, are *generalizations*, since they form rules for the proper use of materials. (2) The existential relation in question is that of means-ends or means-consequences. (3) These propositions in their generalized form may rest upon scientifically warranted empirical propositions and are themselves capable of being tested by observation of results actually attained as compared with those intended.

The objection brought against the view just set forth is that it fails to distinguish between things that are good and right in and of themselves, immediately, intrinsically, and things that are simply good *for* something else. In other words, the latter are useful for attaining the things which have, so it is said, value in and of themselves, since they are prized for their own sake and not as means to something else. This distinction between two different meanings of 'good' (and 'right') is, it is claimed, so crucial for the whole theory of valuation and values that failure to make the distinction destroys the validity of the conclusions that have been set forth. This objection definitely puts before us for consideration the question of the relations to each other of the categories of *means* and *end*. In terms of the dual meaning of 'valuation' already mentioned, the question of the relation of *prizing* and *appraising* to one another is explicitly raised. For, according to the objection, appraising applies only to *means*, while prizing applies to things that are *ends*, so that a difference must be recognized between valuation in its full pregnant sense and evaluation as a secondary and derived affair.

Let the connection between prizing and valuation be admitted and also the connection between desire (and interest) and prizing. The problem as to the relation between appraisal of things as means and prizing of things as ends then takes the following form: Are desires and interests ('likings,' if one prefers that word), which directly effect an institution of end-values, independent of the appraisal of things as means or are they intimately influenced by this appraisal? If a person, for example, finds after due investigation that an immense amount of effort is required to procure the conditions that are the means required for realization of a desire (including perhaps sacrifice of other end-values that might be obtained by the same expenditure of effort), does that fact react to modify his original desire and hence, by definition, his valuation? A survey of what takes place in any deliberate activity provides an affirmative answer to this question. For what is deliberation except weighing of various alternative desires (and hence end-values) in terms of the conditions that are the means of their execution, and which, as means, determine the consequences actually arrived at? There can be no control of the operation of foreseeing consequences (and hence of forming ends-in-view) save in terms of conditions that operate as the causal conditions of their attainment. The proposition in which any object adopted as an end-in-view is statable (or explicitly stated) is *warranted* in just the degree to which existing conditions have been surveyed and appraised in their capacity as means. The sole alternative to this statement is that no deliberation whatsoever occurs, no ends-in-view are formed, but a person acts directly upon whatever impulse happens to present itself.

Any survey of the experiences in which ends-in-view are

formed, and in which earlier impulsive tendencies are shaped through deliberation into a *chosen* desire, reveals that the object finally valued as an end to be reached is determined in its concrete makeup by appraisal of existing conditions as means. However, the habit of completely separating the conceptions of ends from that of means is so ingrained because of a long philosophical tradition that further discussion is required.

1. The common assumption that there is a sharp separation between things, on the one hand, as useful or helpful, and, on the other hand, as *intrinsically* good, and hence that there exists a separation between propositions as to what is expedient, prudent, or advisable and what is inherently desirable, does not, in any case, state a *self-evident* truth. The fact that such words as 'prudent,' 'sensible,' and 'expedient,' in the long run, or after survey of all conditions, merge so readily into the word 'wise' suggests (though, of course, it does not prove) that ends framed in separation from consideration of things as means are foolish to the point of irrationality.

2. Common sense regards some desires and interests as shortsighted, "blind," and others, in contrast, as enlightened, farsighted. It does not for a moment lump all desires and interests together as having the same status with respect to end-values. Discrimination between their respective shortsightedness and farsightedness is made precisely on the ground of whether the object of a given desire is viewed as, in turn, itself a conditioning means of further consequences. Instead of taking a laudatory view of "immediate" desires and valuations, common sense treats refusal to mediate as the very essence of short-view judgment. For treating the end as *merely* immediate and exclusively final is equivalent to refusal to consider what will happen after and because a particular end is reached.

3. The words 'inherent,' 'intrinsic,' and 'immediate' are used ambiguously, so that a fallacious conclusion is reached. Any quality or property that actually belongs to any object or event is properly said to be immediate, inherent, or intrinsic. The fallacy consists in interpreting what is designated by these terms as out of relation to anything else and hence as absolute.

For example, *means* are by definition relational, mediated, and mediating, since they are intermediate between an existing situation and a situation that is to be brought into existence by their use. But the relational character of the *things* that are employed as means does not prevent the things from having their own immediate qualities. In case the things in question are prized and cared for, then, according to the theory that connects the property of value with prizing, they necessarily have an immediate quality of value. The notion that, when means and instruments are valued, the value-qualities which result are only instrumental is hardly more than a bad pun. There is nothing in the nature of prizing or desiring to prevent their being directed to things which are means, and there is nothing in the nature of means to militate against their being desired and prized. In empirical fact, the measure of the value a person attaches to a given end is not what he *says* about its preciousness but the care he devotes to obtaining and using the *means* without which it cannot be attained. No case of notable achievement can be cited in any field (save as a matter of sheer accident) in which the persons who brought about the end did not give loving care to the instruments and agencies of its production. The dependence of ends attained upon means employed is such that the statement just made reduces in fact to a tautology. Lack of desire and interest are proved by neglect of, and indifference to, required means. As soon as an attitude of desire and interest has been developed, then, because without full-hearted attention an end which is professedly prized will not be attained, the desire and interest in question automatically attach themselves to whatever other things are seen to be required means of attaining the end.

The considerations that apply to 'immediate' apply also to 'intrinsic' and 'inherent.' A quality, including that of value, is inherent if it actually belongs to something, and the question of whether or not it belongs is one of *fact* and not a question that can be decided by dialectical manipulation of the concept of inherency. If one has an ardent desire to obtain certain things as means, then the quality of value belongs to, or inheres in, those things. For the time being, producing or obtaining those means *is* the end-in-view. The notion that only that which is out of relation to everything else can justly be called *inherent* is not only itself absurd but is contradicted by the very theory that connects the value of objects as ends with desire and interest, for this view expressly makes the value of the end-object relational, so that, if the inherent is identified with the nonrelational, there are, according to this view, no inherent values at all. On the other hand, if it is the fact that the quality exists in this case, because that to which it belongs is conditioned by a relation, then the relational character of means cannot be brought forward as evidence that their value is not inherent. The same considerations apply to the terms 'intrinsic' and 'extrinsic' as applied to value-qualities. Strictly speaking, the phrase 'extrinsic value' involves a contradiction in terms. Relational properties do not lose their intrinsic quality of being just what they are because their coming into being is *caused* by something 'extrinsic.' The theory that such is the case would terminate logically in the view that there are no intrinsic qualities whatever, since it can be shown that such intrinsic qualities as *red, sweet, hard*, etc., are causally conditioned as to their occurrence. The trouble, once more, is that a dialectic of concepts has taken the place of examination of actual empirical facts. The extreme instance of the view that to be intrinsic is to be out of any relation is found in those writers who hold that, since values *are* intrinsic, they cannot depend upon *any* relation whatever, and certainly not upon a relation to human beings. Hence this school attacks those who connect value-properties with desire and interest on exactly the same ground that the latter equate the distinction between the values of means and ends with the distinction between instrumental and intrinsic values. The views of this extreme nonnaturalistic school may, accordingly, be regarded as a definite exposure of what happens when an analysis of the abstract concept of 'intrinsicalness' is substituted for analysis of empirical occurrences.

The more overtly and emphatically the valuation of objects as ends is connected with desire and interest, the more evident it should be that, since desire and interest are ineffectual save as they co-operatively interact with environing conditions, valuation of desire and interest, as means correlated with other means, is the sole condition for valid appraisal of objects as ends. If the lesson were learned that the object of scientific knowledge is *in any case* an ascertained correlation of changes, it would be seen, beyond the possibility of denial, that anything taken *as end* is in its own content or constituents a correlation of the energies, personal and extra-personal, which operate as means. An end as an *actual* consequence, as an existing outcome, is, like any other occurrence which is scientifically analyzed, nothing but the interaction of the conditions that bring it to pass. Hence it follows necessarily that the *idea* of the object of desire and interest, the *end-in-view* as distinct from the end or outcome actually effected, is warranted in the precise degree in which it is formed in terms of these operative conditions.

4. The chief weakness of current theories of valuation which relate the latter to desire and interest is due to failure to make an empirical analysis of concrete desires and interests as they actually exist. When such an analysis is made, certain relevant considerations at once present themselves.

(i) Desires are subject to frustration and interests are subject to defeat. The likelihood of the occurrence of failure in attaining desired ends is in direct ratio to failure to form desire and interest (and the objects they involve) on the basis of conditions that operate either as obstacles (negatively valued) or as positive resources. The difference between reasonable and unreasonable desires and interests is precisely the difference between those which arise casually and are not reconstituted through consideration of the conditions that will actually decide the outcome and those which are formed on the basis of existing liabilities and potential resources. That desires as they first present themselves are the product of a mechanism consisting of native organic tendencies and acquired habits is an undeniable fact. All growth in maturity consists in *not* immediately giving way to such tendencies but in remaking them in their first manifestation through consideration of the consequences they will occasion *if* they are acted upon—an operation which is equivalent to judging or evaluating them as means operating in connection with extra-personal conditions as also means. Theories of valuation which relate it to desire and interest cannot both eat their cake and have it. They cannot continually oscillate between a view of desire and interest that identifies the latter with impulses just as they happen to occur (as products of organic mechanisms) and a view of desire as a modification of a raw impulse through foresight of its outcome; the latter alone being desire, the whole difference between impulse and desire is made by the presence in desire of an end-in-view, of objects *as* foreseen consequences. The foresight will be dependable in the degree in which it is constituted by examination of the conditions that will in fact decide the outcome. If it seems that this point is being hammered in too insistently, it is because the issue at stake is nothing other and nothing less than the possibility of distinctive valuation-propositions. For it cannot be denied that propositions having evidential warrant and experimental test are possible in the case of evaluation of things as means. Hence it follows that, if these propositions enter into the formation of the interests and desires which are valuations of ends, the latter are thereby constituted the subject matter of authentic empirical affirmations and denials.

(ii) We commonly speak of "learning from experience" and the "maturity" of an individual or a group. What do we mean by such expressions? At the very least, we mean that in the history of individual persons and of the human race there takes place a change from original, comparatively unreflective, impulses and hard-and-fast habits to desires and interests that incorporate the results of critical inquiry. When this process is examined, it is seen to take place chiefly on the basis of careful observation of differences found between desired and proposed ends (ends-*in-view*) and attained ends or actual consequences. Agreement between what is wanted and anticipated and what is actually obtained confirms the selection of conditions which operate as means to the desired end; discrepancies, which are experienced as frustrations and defeats, lead to an inquiry to discover the causes of failure. This inquiry consists of more and more thorough examination of the conditions under which impulses and habits are formed and in which they operate. The result is formation of desires and interests which are what they are through the union of the affective-motor conditions of action with the intellectual or ideational. The latter is there in any case if there is an end-in-view of any sort, no matter how casually formed, while it is adequate in just the degree in which the end is constituted in terms of the conditions of its actualization. For, wherever there is an *end-in-view* of any sort whatever, there is affective-*ideational*-motor activity; or, in terms of the dual meaning of valuation, there is union of prizing and appraising. Observation of results obtained, of *actual* consequences in their agreement with and difference from ends anticipated or held in view, thus provides the conditions by which desires and interests (and hence valuations) are matured and tested. Nothing more contrary to common sense can be imagined than the notion that we are incapable of changing our desires and interests by means of learning what the consequences of acting upon them are, or, as it is sometimes put, of *indulging* them. It should not be necessary to point in evidence to the spoiled child and the adult who cannot "face reality." Yet, as far as valuation and the theory of values are concerned, any theory which isolates valuation of ends from appraisal of means equates the spoiled child and the irresponsible adult to the mature and sane person.

(iii) Every person in the degree in which he is capable of learning from experience draws a distinction between what is desired and what is desirable whenever he engages in formation and choice of competing desires and interests. There is nothing far-fetched or "moralistic" in this statement. The contrast referred to is simply that between the object of a desire as it first presents itself (because of the existing mechanism of impulses and habits) and the object of desire which emerges as a revision of the first-appearing impulse, after the latter is critically judged in reference to the conditions which will decide the actual result. The "desirable," or the object which *should* be desired (valued), does not descend out of the a priori blue nor descend as an imperative from a moral Mount Sinai. It presents itself because past experience has shown that hasty action upon uncriticized desire leads to defeat and possibly to catastrophe. The "desirable" as distinct from the "desired" does not then designate something at large or a priori. It points to the difference between the operation and consequences of unexamined impulses and those of desires and interests that are the product of investigation of conditions and consequences. Social conditions and pressures are part of the conditions that affect the execution of desires. Hence they have to be taken into account in framing ends in terms of available means. But the distinction between the "is" in the sense of the object of a casually emerging desire and the "should be" of a desire framed in relation to actual conditions is a distinction which in any case is bound to offer itself as human beings grow in maturity and part with the childish disposition to "indulge" every impulse as it arises.

Desires and interests are, as we have seen, themselves causal conditions of results. As such they are potential means and have to be appraised as such. This statement is but a restatement of points already made. But it is worth making because it forcibly indicates how far away some of the theoretical views of valuation are from practical common-sense attitudes and beliefs. There is an indefinite number of proverbial sayings which in effect set forth the necessity of not treating desires and interests as final in their first appearance but of treating them as means—that is, of appraising them and forming objects or ends-in-view on the ground of what consequences they will tend to produce in practice. "Look before you leap"; "Act in haste, repent at leisure"; "A stitch in time saves nine"; "When angry count ten"; "Do not put your hand to the plow until the cost has been counted"—are but a few of the many maxims. They are summed up in the old saying, "*Respice finem*"—a saying which marks the difference between simply *having* an end-in-view for which *any* desires suffices, and *looking*, examining, to make sure that the consequences that will actually result are such as will be actually prized and valued when they occur. Only the exigencies of a preconceived theory (in all probability one seriously infected by the conclusions of an uncritically accepted "subjectivistic" psychology) will ignore the concrete differences that are made in the content of "likings" and "prizings," and of desires and interests, by evaluating them in their respective causal capacities when they are taken as means.

V. Ends and Values

It has been remarked more than once that the source of the trouble with theories which relate value to desire and interest, and then proceed to make a sharp division between prizing and appraisal, between ends and means, is the failure to make an empirical investigation of the actual conditions under which desires and interests arise and function, and in which end-objects, ends-in-view, acquire their actual contents. Such an analysis will now be undertaken.

When we inquire into the actual emergence of desire and its object and the value-property ascribed to the latter (instead of merely manipulating dialectically the general concept of desire), it is as plain as anything can be that desires arise only when "there is something the matter," when there is some "trouble" in an existing situation. When analyzed, this "something the matter" is found to spring from the fact that there is something lacking, wanting, in the existing situation as it stands, an absence which produces conflict in the elements that do exist. When things are going completely smoothly, desires do not arise, and there is no occasion to project ends-in-view, for "going smoothly" signifies that there is no need for effort and struggle. It suffices to let things take their "natural" course. There is no occasion to investigate what it would be better to have happen in the future, and hence no projection of an end-object.

Now vital impulses and acquired habits often operate without the intervention of an end-in-view or a purpose. When someone finds that his foot has been stepped on, he is likely to react with a push to get rid of the offending element. He does not stop to form a definite desire and set up an end to be reached. A man who has started walking may continue walking from force of an acquired habit without continually interrupting his course of action to inquire what object is to be obtained at the next step. These rudimentary examples are typical of much of human activity. Behavior is often so direct that no desires and ends intervene and no valuations take place. Only the requirements of a preconceived theory will lead to the conclusion that a hungry animal seeks food because it has formed an idea of an end-object to be reached, or because it has evaluated that object in terms of a desire. Organic tensions suffice to keep the animal going until it has found the material that relieves the tension. But if and when *desire* and *an end-in-view* intervene between the occurrence of a vital impulse or a habitual tendency and the execution of an activity, then the impulse or tendency is to some degree modified and transformed: a statement which is purely tautological, since the occurrence of a desire related to an end-in-view *is* a transformation of a prior impulse or routine habit. It is only in such cases that valuation occurs. This fact, as we have seen, is of much greater importance than it might at first sight seem to be in connection with the theory which relates valuation to desire and interest,[1] for it proves that valuation takes place only when there is something the matter; when there is some trouble to be done away with, some need, lack, or privation to be made good, some conflict of tendencies to be resolved by means of changing existing conditions. This fact in turn proves that there is present an intellectual factor—a factor of inquiry—whenever there is valuation, for the end-in-view is formed and projected as that which, if acted upon, will supply the existing need or lack and resolve the existing conflict. It follows from this that the difference in different desires and their correlative ends-in-view depends upon two things. The first is the adequacy with which inquiry into the lacks and conflicts of the existing situa-

[1] Cf. pp. 29 ff., above.

tion has been carried on. The second is the adequacy of the inquiry into the likelihood that the particular end-in-view which is set up will, if acted upon, actually fill the existing need, satisfy the requirements constituted by what is needed, and do away with conflict by directing activity so as to institute a unified state of affairs.

The case is empirically and dialectically so simple that it would be extremely difficult to understand why it has become so confused in discussion were it not for the influence of irrelevant theoretical preconceptions drawn in part from introspectionist psychology and in part from metaphysics. Empirically, there are two alternatives. Action may take place with or without an end-in-view. In the latter case, there is overt action with no intermediate valuation; a vital impulse or settled habit reacts directly to some immediate sensory stimulation. In case an end-in-view exists and is valued, or exists in relation to a desire or an interest, the (motor) activity engaged in is, tautologically, mediated by the anticipation of the consequences which *as a foreseen end* enter into the makeup of the desire or interest. Now, as has been so often repeated, things can be anticipated or foreseen *as ends* or outcomes only in terms of the conditions by which they are brought into existence. It is simply impossible to have an end-in-view or to anticipate the consequences of any proposed line of action save upon the basis of some, however slight, consideration of the means by which it can be brought into existence. Otherwise, there is no genuine desire but an idle fantasy, a futile wish. That vital impulses and acquired habits are capable of expending themselves in the channels of daydreaming and building castles in the air is unfortunately true. But by description the contents of dreams and air castles are *not* ends-in-view, and what makes them fantasies is precisely the fact that they are *not* formed in terms of actual conditions serving as means of their actualization. *Propositions in which things (acts and materials) are appraised as means enter necessarily into desires and interests that determine end-values.* Hence the importance of the inquiries that result in the appraisal of things as means.

The case is so clear that, instead of arguing it directly, it will prove more profitable to consider how it is that there has grown up the belief that there are such things as ends having value apart from valuation of the means by which they are reached.

1. The mentalistic psychology which operates "to reduce" affective-motor activities to mere *feelings* has also operated in the interpretations assigned to *ends-in-view, purposes,* and *aims.* Instead of being treated as anticipations of consequences of the same order as a prediction of future events and, in any case, as depending for their contents and validity upon such predictions, they have been treated as merely mental states; for, when they are so taken (and only then), ends, needs, and satisfactions are affected in a way that distorts the whole theory of valuation. An end, aim, or purpose as a *mental* state *is* independent of the biological and physical means by which it can be realized. The want, lack, or privation which exists wherever there is desire is then interpreted as a mere state of "mind" instead of as something lacking or absent *in the situation*—something that must be supplied if the empirical situation is to be complete. In its latter sense, the needful or required is that which is *existentially necessary* if an end-in-view is to be brought into actual existence. *What* is needed cannot in this case be told by examination of a state of mind but only by examination of actual conditions. With respect to interpretation of "satisfaction" there is an obvious difference between it as a state of mind and as fulfilment of conditions, i.e., as something that meets the conditions imposed by the conjoint potentialities and lacks of the situation in which desire arises and functions. Satisfaction of desire signifies that the lack, characteristic of the situation evoking desire, has been so met that the means used make sufficient, in the most literal sense, the conditions for accomplishing the end. Because of the subjectivistic interpretation of end, need, and satisfaction, the verbally correct statement that valuation is a *relation* between a personal attitude and extra-personal things—a relation which, moreover, includes a motor (and hence physical) element—is so construed

as to involve separation of means and end, of appraisal and prizing. A "value" is then affirmed to be a "feeling"—a feeling which is not, apparently, the feeling of anything but itself. If it were said that a "value" is *felt*, the statement *might* be interpreted to signify that a certain existing relation between a personal motor attitude and extra-personal environing conditions is a matter of direct experience.

2. The shift of ground between valuation as *desire-interest* and as *enjoyment* introduces further confusion in theory. The shift is facilitated because in fact there exist both enjoyments of things directly possessed *without* desire and effort and enjoyments of things that are possessed only *because* of activity put forth to obtain the conditions required to satisfy desire. In the latter case, the enjoyment is in functional relation to desire or interest, and there is no violation of the definition of valuation in terms of desire-interest. But since the same *word*, 'enjoyment,' is applied also to gratifications that arise quite independently of prior desire and attendant effort, the ground is shifted so that "valuing" is identified with any and every state of enjoyment no matter how it comes about—including gratifications obtained in the most casual and accidental manner, "accidental" in the sense of coming about apart from desire and intent. Take, for example, the gratification of learning that one has been left a fortune by an unknown relative. There is *enjoyment*. But if valuation is defined in terms of desire and interest, there is no valuation, and in so far no "value," the latter coming into being only when there arises some desire as to what shall be done with the money and some question as to formation of an end-in-view. The two kinds of enjoyment are thus not only different but their respective bearings upon the theory of valuation are incompatible with each other, since one is connected with direct possession and the other is conditioned upon prior lack of possession—the very case in which desire enters.

For sake of emphasis, let us repeat the point in a slightly varied illustration. Consider the case of a man gratified by the unexpected receipt of a sum of money, say money picked up while he is walking on the street, an act having nothing to do with his purpose and desire at the moment he is performing it. If values are connected with desire in such a way that the connection is involved in their definition, there is, so far, no valuation. The latter begins when the finder begins to consider *how* he shall prize and care for the money. Shall he prize it, for example, as a means of satisfying certain wants he has previously been unable to satisfy, or shall be prize it as something held in trust until the owner is found? In either case, there is, by definition, an act of valuation. But it is clear that the property of value is attached in the two cases to very different objects. Of course, the uses to which money is put, the ends-in-view which it will serve, are fairly standardized, and in so far the instance just cited is not especially well chosen. But take the case of a child who has found a bright smooth stone. His sense of touch and of sight is gratified. But there is no valuation because no desire and no end-in-view, until the question arises of what shall be done with it; until the child *treasures* what he has accidentally hit upon. The moment he begins to prize and care for it he puts it to some use and thereby employs it as a *means* to some end, and, depending upon his maturity, he estimates or values it *in that relation*, or as means to end.

The confusion that occurs in theory when shift is made from valuation related to desire and interest, to "enjoyment" independent of any relation to desire and interest is facilitated by the fact that attainment of the objectives of desire and interest (of valuation) is itself enjoyed. The nub of the confusion consists in isolating enjoyment from the conditions under which it occurs. Yet the enjoyment that is the consequence of fulfilment of a desire and realization of an interest is what it is because of satisfaction or making good of a need or lack—a satisfaction conditioned by effort directed by the idea of something as an end-in-view. In this sense "enjoyment" involves inherent connection with *lack* of possession; while, in the other sense, the "enjoyment" is that of sheer possession. Lack of possession and possession are tautologically incompatible. Moreover, it is a common experience that the object of desire when attained is *not* enjoyed, so common that there are proverbial sayings to the effect that enjoyment is in the seeking rather than in the obtaining. It is not necessary to take these sayings literally to be aware that the occurrences in question prove the existence of the difference between value as connected with desire and value as mere enjoyment. Finally, as matter of daily experience, enjoyments provide the primary material of *problems* of valuation. Quite independently of any "moral" issues, people continually ask themselves whether a given enjoyment is worth while or whether the conditions involved in its production are such as to make it a costly indulgence.

Reference was made earlier to the confusion in theory which results when "values" are *defined* in terms of vital impulses. (The ground offered is that the latter are conditions of the existence of values in the sense that they "spring from" vital impulse.) In the text from which the passage was quoted there occurs in close connection the following: "The ideal of rationality is itself as arbitrary, as much dependent upon the needs of a finite organization, as any other ideal." Implicit in this passage are two extraordinary conceptions. One of them is that an ideal is arbitrary if it is causally conditioned by actual existences and is relevant to actual needs of human beings. This conception is extraordinary because naturally it would be supposed that an ideal is arbitrary in the degree in which it is *not* connected with things which exist and is not related to concrete existential requirements. The other astounding conception is that the ideal of rationality is "arbitrary" because it is so conditioned. One would suppose it to be peculiarly true of the ideal of rationality that it is to be judged as to its reasonableness (versus its arbitrariness) on the ground of its function, of what it does, not on the ground of its origin. If rationality as an ideal or generalized end-in-view serves to direct conduct so that things experienced in consequence of conduct so directed are more reasonable in the concrete, nothing more can be asked of it. Both of the implied conceptions are so extraordinary that they can be understood only on the ground of some unexpressed preconceptions. As far as one can judge, these preconceptions are (i) that an ideal *ought* to be independent of existence, that is, a priori. The reference to the origin of ideals in vital impulses is in fact an effective criticism of this a priori view. But it provides a ground for calling ideas arbitrary only if the a priori view is accepted. (ii) The other preconception would seem to be an acceptance of the view that there are or ought to be "ends-in-themselves"; that is to say, ends or ideals that are not also means, which, as we have already seen, is precisely what an ideal is, if it is judged and valued in terms of its function. The sole way of arriving at the conclusion that a generalized end-in-view or ideal is arbitrary because of existential and empirical origin is by first laying down as an ultimate criterion that an end should also *not* be a means. The whole passage and the views of which it is a typical and influential manifestation is redolent of the survival of belief in "ends-in-themselves" as the solely and finally legitimate kind of ends.

VI. The Continuum of Ends-Means

Those who have read and enjoyed Charles Lamb's essay on the origin of roast pork have probably not been conscious that their enjoyment of its absurdity was due to perception of the absurdity of any "end" which is set up apart from the means by which it is to be attained and apart from its own further function as means. Nor is it probable that Lamb himself wrote the story as a deliberate travesty of the theories that make such a separation. Nonetheless, that is the whole point of the tale. The story, it will be remembered, is that roast pork was first enjoyed when a house in which pigs were confined was accidentally burned down. While searching in the ruins, the owners touched the pigs that had been roasted in the fire and scorched their fingers. Impulsively bringing their fingers to their mouths to cool them, they experienced a new taste. Enjoying the taste, they henceforth set themselves to building houses, inclosing pigs in them, and then burning the houses down. Now, if ends-in-view are what they are entirely apart from means, and have their value independently of valuation of means, there is nothing absurd, nothing ridiculous, in this procedure, for the end attained, the *de facto* termination, *was* eating and enjoying roast pork, and that was just the end desired. Only when the end attained is estimated in terms of the means employed—the building and burning-down of houses in comparison with other available means by which the desired result in view might be attained—is there anything absurd or unreasonable about the method employed.

The story has a direct bearing upon another point, the meaning of 'intrinsic.' *Enjoyment* of the taste of roast pork may be said to be immediate, although even so the enjoyment would be a somewhat troubled one, for those who have memory, by the thought of the needless cost at which it was obtained. But to pass from immediacy of enjoyment to something called "intrinsic value" is a leap for which there is no ground. The *value* of enjoyment of an object *as* an attained end is a value of something which in being an end, an outcome, stands in relation to the means of which it is the consequence. Hence if the object in question is prized *as* an end or "final" value, it is valued *in this relation* or as mediated. The first time roast pork was enjoyed, it was *not* an end-value, since by description it was not the result of desire, foresight, and intent. Upon subsequent occasions it was, by description, the outcome of prior foresight, desire, and effort, and hence occupied the position of an end-in-view. There are occasions in which previous effort enhances enjoyment of what is attained. But there are also many occasions in which persons find that, when they have attained something as an end, they have paid too high a price in effort and in sacrifice of other ends. In such situations *enjoyment* of the end attained is itself *valued*, for it is not taken in its immediacy but in terms of its cost—a fact fatal to its being regarded as "an end-in-itself," a self-contradictory term in any case.

The story throws a flood of light upon what is usually meant by the maxim "the end justifies the means" and also upon the popular objection to it. Applied in this case, it would mean that the value of the attained end, the eating of roast pork, was such as to warrant the price paid in the means by which it was attained—destruction of dwelling-houses and sacrifice of the values to which they contribute. The conception involved in the maxim that "the end justifies the means" is basically the same as that in the notion of ends-in-themselves; indeed, from a historical point of view, it is the fruit of the latter, for only the conception that certain things are ends-in-themselves can warrant the belief that the relation of ends-means is unilateral, proceeding exclusively from end to means. When the maxim is compared with empirically ascertained facts, it is equivalent to holding one of two views, both of which are incompatible with the facts. One of the views is that only the specially selected "end" held in view will actually be brought into existence by the means used, something miraculously intervening to prevent the means employed from having their other usual effects; the other (and more probable) view is that, as compared with the importance of the selected and uniquely prized end, other consequences may be completely ignored and brushed aside no matter how intrinsically obnoxious they are. This arbitrary selection of some one part of the attained consequences as *the* end and hence as the warrant of means used (no matter how objectionable are their *other* consequences) is the fruit of holding that *it*, as *the* end, is an end-in-itself, and hence possessed of "value" irrespective of all its existential relations. And this notion is inherent in *every* view that assumes that "ends" can be valued apart from appraisal of the things used as means in attaining them. The sole alternative to the view that *the* end is an arbitrarily selected part of actual consequences which *as* "the end" then justifies the use of means irrespective of the other consequences they produce, is that desires, ends-in-view, and consequences achieved be valued in turn as means of further consequences. The maxim referred to, under the guise of saying that ends, in the sense of actual consequences, provide the warrant for means employed—a correct position—actually says that some fragment of these actual consequences—a fragment arbitrarily selected because the heart has been set upon it—authorizes the use of means to obtain *it*, without the need of foreseeing and weighing other ends as consequences of the means used. It thus discloses in a striking manner the fallacy involved in the position that ends have value independent of appraisal of means involved and independent of their own further causal efficacy.

We are thus brought back to a point already set forth. In all the physical sciences (using 'physical' here as a synonym for *nonhuman*) it is now taken for granted that all "effects" are also "causes," or, stated more accurately, that nothing happens which is *final* in the sense that it is not part of an ongoing stream of events.. If this principle, with the accompanying discrediting of belief in objects that are ends but not means, is employed in dealing with distinctive human phenomena, it necessarily follows that the distinction between ends and means is temporal and relational. Every condition that has to be brought into existence in order to serve as means is, *in that connection*, an object of desire and an end-in-view, while the end actually reached is a means to future ends as well as a test of valuations previously made. Since the end attained is a condition of further existential occurrences, it must be appraised as a potential obstacle and potential resource. If the notion of some objects as ends-in-themselves were abandoned, not merely in words but in all practical implications, human beings would for the first time in history be in a position to frame ends-in-view and form desires on the basis of empirically grounded propositions of the temporal relations of events to one another.

At any given time an adult person in a social group has certain ends which are so standardized by custom that they are taken for granted without examination, so that the only problems arising concern the best means for attaining them. In one group money-making would be such an end; in another group, possession of political power; in another group, advancement of scientific knowledge; in still another group, military prowess, etc. But such ends in any case are (i) more or less blank frameworks where the nominal "end" sets limits within which definite ends will fall, the latter being determined by appraisal of things as means; while (ii) as far as they simply express habits that have become established without critical examination of the relation of means and ends, they do not provide a model for a theory of valuation to follow. If a person moved by an experience of intense cold, which is highly objectionable, should momentarily judge it worth while to get warm by burning his house down, all that saves him from an act determined by a "compulsion neurosis" is the intellectual realization of what other consequences would ensue with the loss of his house. It is not necessarily a sign of insanity (as in the case cited) to isolate some event projected as an end out of the context of a world of moving changes in which it will in fact take place. But it is at least a sign of immaturity when an individual fails to view his end as also a moving condition of further consequences, thereby treating it as *final* in the sense in which 'final' signifies that the course of events has come to a complete stop. Human beings do indulge in such arrests. But to treat them as models for forming a theory of ends is to substitute a manipulation of ideas, abstracted from the contexts in which they arise and function, for the conclusions of observation of concrete facts. It is a sign either of insanity, immaturity, indurated routine, or of a fanaticism that is a mixture of all three.

Generalized ideas of ends and values undoubtedly exist. They exist not only as expressions of habit and as uncritical and probably invalid ideas but also in the same way as valid general ideas arise in any subject. Similar situations recur; desires and interests are carried over from one situation to another and progressively consolidated. A schedule of general ends results, the involved values being "abstract" in the sense of not being directly connected with any particular existing case but not in the sense of independence of all empirically existent cases. As with general ideas in the conduct of any natural science, these general ideas are used as intellectual instrumentalities in judgment of particular cases as the latter arise; they are, in effect, tools that direct and facilitate examination of things in the concrete while they are also developed and tested by the results of their application in these cases. Just as the natural sciences began a course of sure development when the dialectic of concepts ceased to be employed to arrive at conclusions about existential affairs and was employed instead as a means of arriving at a hypothesis fruitfully applicable to particulars, so it will be with the theory of human activities and relations. There is irony in the fact that the very continuity of experienced activities which enables general ideas of value to function as rules for evaluation of particular desires and ends should have become the source of a belief that desires, by the bare fact of their occurrence, confer value upon objects as ends, entirely independent of their contexts in the continuum of activities.

In this connection there is danger that the idea of "finality" be manipulated in a way analogous to the manipulation of the concepts of "immediacy" and "intrinsic" previously remarked upon. A value is *final* in the sense that it represents the conclusion of a process of analytic appraisals of conditions operating in a concrete case, the conditions including impulses and desires on one side and external conditions on the other. Any conclusion reached by an inquiry that is taken to warrant the conclusion is "final" for that case. "Final" here has logical force. The quality or property of value that is correlated with the *last* desire formed in the process of valuation is, tautologically, ultimate for that particular situation. It applies, however, to a specifiable temporal *means-end relation* and not to something which is an end per se. There is a fundamental difference between a final property or quality and the property or quality of finality.

The objection always brought against the view set forth is that, according to it, valuation activities and judgments are involved in a hopeless *regressus ad infinitum.* If, so it is said, there is no end which is not in turn a means, foresight has no place at which it can stop, and no end-in-view can be formed except by the most arbitrary of acts—an act so arbitrary that it mocks the claim of being a genuine valuation-proposition.

This objection brings us back to the conditions under which desires take shape and foreseen consequences are projected as ends to be reached. These conditions are those of need, deficit, and conflict. Apart from a condition of tension between a person and environing conditions there is, as we have seen, no occasion for evocation of desire for something else; there is nothing to induce the formation of an end, much less the formation of one end rather than any other out of the indefinite number of ends theoretically possible. Control of transformation of active tendencies into a desire in which a particular end-in-view is incorporated, is exercised by the needs or privations of an actual situation as its requirements are disclosed to observation. The "value" of different ends that suggest themselves is estimated or measured by the capacity they exhibit to guide action in making good, *satisfying*, in its literal sense, existing lacks. Here is the factor which cuts short the process of foreseeing and weighing ends-in-view in their function as means. Sufficient unto the day is the evil thereof and sufficient also is the *good* of that which does away with the existing evil. Sufficient because it is the means of instituting a complete situation or an integrated set of conditions.

Two illustrations will be given. A physician has to determine the value of various courses of action and their results in the case of a particular patient. He forms ends-in-view having the value that justifies their adoption, on the ground of what his examination discloses is the "matter" or "trouble" with the patient. He estimates the worth of what he undertakes on the ground of its capacity to produce a condition in which these troubles will not exist, in which, as it is ordinarily put, the patient will be "restored to health." He does not have an idea of health as an absolute end-in-itself, an absolute good by which to determine what to do. On the contrary, he forms his general idea of health as an end and a good (value) for the patient on the ground of what his techniques of examination have shown to be the troubles from which patients suffer and the means by which they are overcome. There is no need to deny that a general and abstract conception of health finally develops. But it is the outcome of a great number of definite, empirical inquiries, not an a priori preconditioning "standard" for carrying on inquiries.

The other illustration is more general. In all inquiry, even the most completely scientific, what is proposed as a conclusion (the end-in-view in that inquiry) is evaluated as to its worth on the ground of its ability to resolve the *problem* presented by the conditions under investigation. There is no a priori standard for determining the value of a proposed solution in concrete cases. A hypothetical possible solution, as an end-in-view, is used as a methodological means to direct further observations and experiments. Either it performs the function of resolution of a problem for the sake of which it is adopted and tried or it does not. Experience has shown that problems for the most part fall into certain recurrent kinds so that there are general principles which, it is believed, proposed solutions must satisfy in a particular case. There thus develops a sort of framework of conditions to be satisfied—a framework of reference which operates in an *empirically* regulative way in given cases. We may even say that it operates as an "a priori" principle, but in exactly the same sense in which rules for the conduct of a technological art are both empirically antecedent and controlling in a given case of the art. While there is no a priori standard of health with which the actual state of human beings can be compared so as to determine whether they are well or ill, or in what respect they are ill, there have developed, out of past experience, certain criteria which are operatively applicable in new cases as they arise. Ends-in-view are appraised or valued as *good* or *bad* on the ground of their serviceability in the direction of behavior dealing with states of affairs found to be objectionable because of some lack or conflict in them. They are appraised as fit or unfit, proper or improper, *right* or *wrong*, on the ground of their *requiredness* in accomplishing this end.

Considering the all but omnipresence of troubles and "evils" in human experience (evils in the sense of deficiencies, failures, and frustrations), and considering the amount of time that has been spent explaining them away, theories of human activity have been strangely oblivious of the concrete function troubles are capable of exercising when they are taken as *problems* whose conditions and consequences are explored with a view to finding methods of solution. The two instances just cited, the progress of medical art and of scientific inquiry, are most instructive on this point. As long as actual events were supposed to be judged by comparison with some absolute end-value as a standard and norm, no sure progress was made. When standards of health and of satisfaction of conditions of knowledge were conceived in terms of analytic observation of existing conditions, disclosing a trouble statable in a problem, criteria of judging were progressively self-corrective through the very process of use in observation to locate the source of the trouble and to indicate the effective means of dealing with it. These means form the content of the specific end-in-view, not some abstract standard or ideal.

This emphasis upon the function of needs and conflicts as the controlling factor in institution of ends and values does not signify that the latter are themselves negative in content and import. While they are framed with reference to a negative factor, deficit, want, privation, and conflict, their function is positive, and the resolution effected by performance of their function is positive. To attempt to gain an end *directly* is to put into operation the very conditions that are the source of the experienced trouble, thereby strengthening them and at most changing the outward form in which they manifest themselves. Ends-in-view framed with a negative *reference* (i.e., to some trouble or problem) are means which inhibit the operation of conditions producing the obnoxious result; they enable positive conditions to operate as resources and thereby to effect a result which is, in the highest possible sense, positive in content. The content of the end as an object *held in view* is intellectual or methodological; the content of the attained outcome or the end *as consequence* is existential. It is positive in the degree in which it marks the doing-away of the need and conflict that evoked the *end-in-view*. The negative factor operates as a condition of forming the appropriate *idea* of an end; the idea when acted upon determines a positive outcome.

The attained end or consequence is always an organization of activities, where organization is a co-ordination of all activities which enter as factors. The *end-in-view* is that particular activity which operates as a co-ordinating factor of all other subactivities involved. Recognition of the end as a co-ordination or unified organization of activities, and of the end-in-view as the special activity which is the means of effecting this co-ordination, does away with any appearance of paradox that seems to be attached to the idea of a temporal continuum of activities in which each successive stage is equally end and means. The *form* of an attained end or consequence is always the same: that of adequate co-ordination. The content or involved matter of each successive result differs from that of its predecessors; for, while it is a *reinstatement* of a unified ongoing action, after a period of interruption through conflict and need, it is also an *enactment* of a new state of affairs. It has the qualities and properties appropriate to its being the consummatory resolution of a previous state of activity in which there was a peculiar need, desire, and end-in-view. In the continuous temporal process of organizing activities into a co-ordinated and co-ordinating unity, a constituent activity is both an end and a means: an end, in so far as it is temporally and relatively a close; a means, in so far as it provides a condition to be taken into account in further activity.

Instead of there being anything strange or paradoxical in the existence of situations in which means are constituents of the very end-objects they have helped to bring into existence, such situations occur whenever behavior succeeds in intelligent projection of ends-in-view that direct activity to resolution of the antecedent trouble. The cases in which ends and means fall apart are the abnormal ones, the ones which deviate from activity which is intelligently conducted. Wherever, for example, there is sheer drudgery, there is separation of the required and necessary means from both the end-in-view and the end attained. Wherever, on the other side, there is a so-called "ideal" which is utopian and a matter of fantasy, the same separation occurs, now from the side of the so-called *end*. Means that do not become constituent elements of the very ends or consequences they produce form what are called "necessary evils," their "necessity" being relative to the existing state of knowledge and art. They are comparable to scaffoldings that had to be later torn down, but which were necessary in erection of buildings until elevators were introduced. The latter remained for use in the building erected and were employed as means of transporting materials that in turn became an integral part of the building. Results or consequences which at one time were necessarily waste products in the production of the particular thing desired were utilized in the light of the development of human experience and intelligence as means for further desired consequences. The generalized ideal and standard of economy-efficiency which operates in every advanced art and technology is equivalent, upon analysis, to the conception of means that are constituents of ends attained and of ends that are usable as means to further ends.

It must also be noted that *activity* and *activities*, as these words are employed in the foregoing account, involve, like any actual behavior, existential materials, as breathing involves air; walking, the earth; buying and selling, commodities; inquiry, things investigated, etc. No human activity operates in a vacuum; it acts in the world and has materials upon which and through which it produces results. On the other hand, no material—air, water, metal, wood, etc.—is *means* save as it is employed in some human activity to accomplish something. When "organization of activities" is mentioned, it always includes within itself organization of the materials existing in the world in which we live. That organization which is the "final" value for each concrete situation of valuation thus forms part of the existential conditions that have to be taken into account in further formation of desires and interests or valuations. In the degree in which a particular valuation is invalid because of inconsiderate shortsighted investigation of things in their relation of means-end, difficulties are put in the way of subsequent reasonable valuations. To the degree in which desires and interests are formed after critical survey of the conditions which as means determine the actual outcome, the more smoothly continuous become subsequent activities, for consequences attained are then such as are evaluated more readily as means in the continuum of action.

VII. Theory of Valuation as Outline of a Program

Because of the confusion which affects current discussion of the problem of valuation, the analysis undertaken in the present study has been obliged to concern itself to a˙considerable extent with tracking the confusion to its source. This is necessary in order that empirical inquiry into facts which are taken for granted by common sense may be freed from irrelevant and confusing associations. The more important conclusions may be summarized as follows.

1. Even if "value-expressions" were ejaculatory and such as to influence the conduct of other persons, genuine propositions about such expressions would be possible. We could investigate whether or not they had the effect intended; and further examination would be able to discover the differential conditions of the cases that were successful in obtaining the intended outcome and those that were not. It is useful to discriminate between linguistic expressions which are "emotive" and those which are "scientific." Nevertheless, even if the former said nothing whatever, they would, like other natural events, be capable of becoming the subject matter of "scientific" propositions as a result of a examination of their conditions and effects.

2. Another view connects valuation and value-expressions with desires and interests. Since desire and interest are behavioral phenomena (involving at the very least a "motor" aspect), the valuations they produce are capable of being investigated as to *their* respective conditions and results. Valuations are empirically observable patterns of behavior and may be studied as such. The propositions that result are *about* valuations but are not of themselves value-propositions in any sense marking them off from other matter-of-fact propositions.

3. Value-propositions of the distinctive sort exist whenever things are appraised as to their suitability and serviceability as means, for such propositions are not about things or events that have occurred or that already exist (although they cannot be validly instituted apart from propositions of the kind mentioned in the previous sentence), but are about things *to be*

brought into existence. Moreover, while they are logically conditioned upon matter-of-fact predictions, they are more than simple predictions, for the things in question are such as will *not* take place, under the given circumstances, except through the intervention of some personal act. The difference is similar to that between a proposition predicting that in *any* case a certain eclipse will take place and a proposition that the eclipse will be seen or experienced by certain human beings in case the latter intervene to perform certain actions. While valuation-propositions as appraisals of means occur in all arts and technologies and are grounded in strictly physical propositions (as in advanced engineering technologies), nevertheless they are distinct from the latter in that they inherently involve the means-end relationship.

4. Wherever there are desires, there are *ends-in-view*, not simply effects produced as in the case of sheer impulse, appetite, and routine habit. Ends-in-view as anticipated results reacting upon a given desire are *ideational* by definition or tautologically. The involved foresight, forecast or anticipation is warranted, like any other intellectual inferent factor, in the degree in which it is based upon propositions that are conclusions of adequate observational activities. Any given desire is what it is in its actual content or "object" *because* of its ideational constituents. Sheer impulse or appetite may be described as affective-motor; but any theory that connects valuation with desire and interest by that very fact connects valuation with behavior which is affective-*ideational*-motor. This fact proves the *possibility* of the existence of distinctive valuation-propositions. In view of the role played by ends-in-view in directing the activities that contribute either to the realization or to the frustration of desire, the *necessity* for valuation-propositions is proved if desires are to be intelligent, and purposes are to be other than shortsighted and irrational.

5. The required appraisal of desires and ends-in-view, as means of the activities by which actual results are produced, is dependent upon observation of consequences attained when they are compared and contrasted with the content of ends-in-

view. Careless, inconsiderate action is that which foregoes the inquiry that determines the points of agreement and disagreement between the desire actually formed (and hence the valuation actually made) and the things brought into existence by acting upon it. Since desire and valuation of objects proposed as ends are inherently connected, and since desire and ends-in-view need to be appraised as means to ends (an appraisal made on the basis of warranted physical generalizations) the valuation of ends-in-view is tested by consequences that actually ensue. It is verified to the degree in which there is agreement upon results. Failure to agree, in case deviations are carefully observed, is not mere failure but provides the means for improving the formation of later desires and ends-in-view.

The net outcome is (i) that the problem of valuation in general as well as in particular cases concerns things that sustain to one another the relation of means-ends; that (ii) ends are determinable only on the ground of the means that are involved in bringing them about; and that (iii) desires and interests must themselves be evaluated as means in their interaction with external or environing conditions. Ends-in-view, as distinct from ends as accomplished results, themselves function as directive means; or, in ordinary language, as *plans*. Desires, interests, and environing conditions as means are modes of action, and hence are to be conceived in terms of energies which are capable of reduction to homogeneous and comparable terms. Co-ordination or organizations of energies, proceeding from the two sources of the organism and the environment, are thus both means and attained result or "end" in all cases of valuation, the two kinds of energy being theoretically (if not as yet completely so in practice) capable of statement in terms of physical units.

The conclusions stated do not constitute a complete theory of valuation. They do, however, state the conditions which such a theory must satisfy. An actual theory can be completed only when inquiries into things sustaining the relation of ends-means have been systematically conducted and their results brought to bear upon the formation of desires and ends. For the theory of valuation is itself an intellectual or methodological means and as such can be developed and perfected only in and by use. Since that use does not now exist in any adequate way, the theoretical consideration advanced and conclusions reached outline a program to be undertaken, rather than a complete theory. The undertaking can be carried out only by regulated guidance of the formation of interests and purposes in the concrete. The prime condition of this undertaking (in contrast with the current theory of the relation of valuation to desire and interest) is recognition that desire and interest are not given ready-made at the outset, and a fortiori are not, as they may at first appear, starting-points, original data, or premises of any theory of valuation, for desire always emerges within a prior system of activities or interrelated energies. It arises within a *field* when the field is disrupted or is menaced with disruption, when conflict introduces the tension of need or threatens to introduce it. An interest represents not just a desire but a set of interrelated desires which have been found in experience to produce, because of their connection with one another, a definite order in the processes of continuing behavior.

The test of the existence of a valuation and the nature of the latter is actual behavior as that is subject to observation. Is the existing field of activities (including environing conditions) *accepted*, where "acceptance" consists in effort to maintain it against adverse conditions? Or is it *rejected*, where "rejection" consists of effort to get rid of it and to produce another behavioral field? And in the latter case, what is the actual field to which, as an end, desire-efforts (or the organization of desire-efforts constituting an interest) are directed? Determination of this field as an objective of behavior determines *what* is valued. Until there is actual or threatened shock and disturbance of a situation, there is a green light to go ahead in immediate act— overt action. There is no need, no desire, and no valuation, just as where there is no doubt, there is no cause of inquiry. Just as the problem which evokes inquiry is related to an empirical situation in which the problem presents itself, so desire and the projection of ends as consequences to be reached are relative to a concrete situation and to its need for transformation. The burden of proof lies, so to speak, on occurrence of conditions that are impeding, obstructive, and that introduce conflict and need. Examination of the situation in respect to the conditions that constitute lack and need and thus serve as positive means for formation of an attainable end or outcome, is the method by which warranted (required and effective) desires and ends-in-view are formed: by which, in short, valuation takes place.

The confusions and mistakes in existing theories, which have produced the need for the previous prolonged analysis, arise very largely from taking desire and interest as original instead of in the contextual situations in which they arise. When they are so taken, they become ultimate in relation to valuation. Being taken, so to speak, at large, there is nothing by which we can empirically check or test them. If desire were of this original nature, if it were independent of the structure and requirements of some concrete empirical situation and hence had no function to perform with reference to an existential situation, then insistence upon the necessity of an ideational or intellectual factor in every desire and the consequent necessity for fulfilment of the empirical conditions of its validity would be as superfluous and irrelevant as critics have said it is. The insistence might then be, what it has been called, a "moral" bias springing from an interest in the "reform" of individuals and society. But since in empirical fact there are no desires and interests apart from some field of activities in which they occur and in which they function, either as poor or as good means, the insistence in question is simply and wholly in the interest of a correct empirical account of what actually exists as over against what turns out to be, when examined, a dialectical manipulation of *concepts* of desire and interest at large, a procedure which is all that is possible when desire is taken in isolation from its existential context.

It is a common occurrence in the history of theories that an error at one extreme calls out a complementary error at the other extreme. The type of theory just considered isolates desires as sources of valuation from any existential context and hence from any possibility of intellectual control of their contents and objectives. It thereby renders valuation an arbitrary matter. It says in effect that any desire is just as "good" as any other in respect to the value it institutes. Since desires—and their organization into interests—are the sources of human action, this view, if it were systematically acted upon, would produce disordered behavior to the point of complete chaos. The fact that in spite of conflicts, and unnecessary conflicts, there is not complete disorder is proof that actually some degree of intellectual respect for existing conditions and consequences does operate as a control factor in formation of desires and valuations. However, the implications of the theory in the direction of intellectual and practical disorder are such as to evoke a contrary theory, one, however, which has the same fundamental postulate of the isolation of valuation from concrete empirical situations, their potentialities, and their requirements. This is the theory of "ends-in-themselves" as ultimate standards of all valuation—a theory which denies implicitly or explicitly that desires have anything to do with "final values" unless and until they are subjected to the external control of a priori absolute ends as standards and ideals for their valuation. This theory, in its endeavor to escape from the frying pan of disordered valuations, jumps into the fire of absolutism. It confers the simulation of final and complete rational authority upon certain interests of certain persons or groups at the expense of all others: a view which, in turn, because of the consequences it entails, strengthens the notion that no intellectual and empirically reasonable control of desires, and hence of valuations and value-properties, is possible. The seesaw between theories which by definition are not empirically testable (since they are a priori) and professed empirical theories that unwittingly substitute conclusions derived from the bare *concept* of desire for the results of observation of desires in the concrete is thus kept up. The astonishing thing about the a priori theory (astonishing if the history of philosophical thought be omitted from the survey) is its complete neglect of the fact that valuations are constant phenomena of human behavior, personal and associated, and are capable of rectification and development by use of the resources provided by knowledge of physical relations.

VIII. Valuation and the Conditions of Social Theory

We are thus brought to the problem which, as was shown in the opening section of this study, is back of the present interest in the problem of valuation and values, namely, the possibility of genuine and grounded propositions about the purposes, plans, measures, and policies which influence human activity whenever the latter is other than merely impulsive or routine. A theory of valuation *as* theory can only set forth the conditions which a method of formation of desires and interests must observe in concrete situations. The problem of the existence of such a method is all one with the problem of the possibility of genuine propositions which have as their subject matter the intelligent conduct of human activities, whether personal or associated. The view that value in the sense of *good* is inherently connected with that which promotes, furthers, assists, a course of activity, and that value in the sense of *right* is inherently connected with that which is needed, required, in the maintenance of a course of activity, is not in itself novel. Indeed, it is suggested by the very etymology of the word *value*, associated as it is with the words 'avail,' 'valor,' 'valid,' and 'invalid.' What the foregoing discussion has added to the idea is proof that if, and *only* if, valuation is taken in this sense, are empirically grounded propositions about desires and interests as sources of valuations possible—such propositions being grounded in the degree in which they employ scientific physical generalizations as means of forming propositions about activities which are correlated as ends-means. The resulting general propositions provide rules for valuation of the aims, purposes, plans, and policies that direct intelligent human activity. They are not rules in the sense that they enable us to tell directly, or upon bare inspection, the values of given particular ends (a foolish quest that underlies the belief in a priori values as ideals and standards); they are rules of methodic procedure in the conduct of the investigations that determine the respective conditions and consequences of various modes of behavior. It does not purport to solve the problems of valuation in and of itself; it does claim to state conditions that inquiry must satisfy if these problems are to be resolved, and to serve in this way as a leading principle in conduct of such inquiries.

I. Valuations exist in fact and are capable of empirical observation so that propositions about them are empirically verifiable. What individuals and groups hold dear or prize and the grounds upon which they prize them are capable, in principle, of ascertainment, no matter how great the *practical* difficulties in the way. But, upon the whole, in the past values have been determined by customs, which are then commended because they favor some special interest, the commendation being attended with coercion or exhortation or with a mixture of both. The practical difficulties in the way of scientific inquiry into valuations are great, so great that they are readily mistaken for inherent theoretical obstacles. Moreover, such knowledge as does exist about valuations is far from organized, to say nothing about its being adequate. The notion that valuations do not exist in empirical fact and that therefore value-conceptions have to be imported from a source outside experience is one of the most curious beliefs the mind of man has ever entertained. Human beings are continuously engaged in valuations. The latter supply the primary material for operations of further valuations and for the general theory of valuation.

Knowledge of these valuations does not of itself, as we have seen, provide valuation-propositions; it is rather of the nature of historical and cultural-anthropological knowledge. But such factual knowledge is a *sine qua non* of ability to formulate valuation-propositions. This statement only involves recognition that past experience, when properly analyzed and ordered, is the sole guide we have in future experience. An individual within the limits of his personal experience revises his desires and purposes as he becomes aware of the consequences they have produced in the past. This knowledge is what enables him to foresee probable consequences of his prospective activities and to direct his conduct accordingly. The ability to form valid propositions about the relation of present desires and purposes to future consequences depends in turn upon ability to analyze these present desires and purposes into their constituent elements. When they are taken in gross, foresight is correspondingly coarse and indefinite. The history of science shows that power of prediction has increased *pari passu* with analysis of gross qualitative events into elementary constituents. Now, in the absence of adequate and organized knowledge of human valuations as occurrences that have taken place, it is a fortiori impossible that there be valid propositions formulating new valuations in terms of consequences of specified causal conditions. On account of the continuity of human activities, personal and associated, the import of present valuations cannot be validly stated until they are placed in the perspective of the past valuation-events with which they are continuous. Without this perception, the future perspective, i.e., the consequences of present and new valuations, is indefinite. In the degree in which existing desires and interests (and hence valuations) can be judged in their connection with past conditions, they are seen in a context which enables them to be revaluated on the ground of evidence capable of observation and empirical test.

Suppose, for example, that it be ascertained that a particular set of current valuations have, as their antecedent historical conditions, the interest of a small group or special class in maintaining certain exclusive privileges and advantages, and that this maintenance has the effect of limiting both the range of the desires of others and their capacity to actualize them. Is it not obvious that this knowledge of conditions and consequences would surely lead to revaluation of the desires and ends that had been assumed to be authoritative sources of valuation? Not that such revaluation would of necessity take effect immediately. But, when valuations that exist at a given time are found to lack the support they have previously been supposed to have, they exist in a context that is highly adverse to their continued maintenance. In the long run the effect is similar to a warier attitude that develops toward certain bodies of water as the result of knowledge that these bodies of water contain disease germs. If, on the other hand, investigation shows that a given set of existing valuations, including the rules for their enforcement, be such as to release individual potentialities of desire and interest, and does so in a way that contributes to mutual reinforcement of the desires and interests of all members of a group, it is impossible for this knowledge not to serve as a bulwark of the particular set of valuations in question, and to induce intensified effort to sustain them in existence.

II. These considerations lead to the central question: What are the conditions that have to be met so that knowledge of past and existing valuations becomes an instrumentality of valuation in formation of new desires and interests—of desires and interests that the test of experience show to be best worth fostering? It is clear upon our view that no abstract theory of valuation can be put side by side, so to speak, with existing valuations as the standard for judging them.

The answer is that improved valuation must grow out of existing valuations, subjected to critical methods of investigation that bring them into systematic relations with one another. Admitting that these valuations are largely and probably, in the main, defective, it might at first sight seem as if the idea that improvement would spring from bringing them into connection with one another is like recommending that one lift himself by his bootstraps. But such an impression arises only because of failure to consider how they actually may be brought into relation with one another, namely, by examination of their respective conditions and consequences. Only by following this path will they be reduced to such homogeneous terms that they are comparable with one another.

This method, in fact, simply carries over to human or social phenomena the methods that have proved successful in dealing with the subject matter of physics and chemistry. In these fields before the rise of modern science there was a mass of facts which were isolated and seemingly independent of one another. Systematic advance dates from the time when conceptions that formed the content of theory were derived from the phenomena themselves and were then employed as hypotheses for relating together the otherwise separate matters-of-fact. When, for example, ordinary drinking water is operatively regarded as H_2O what has happened is that water is related to an immense number of other phenomena so that inferences and predictions are indefinitely expanded and, at the same time, made subject to empirical tests. In the field of human activities there are at present an immense number of facts of desires and purposes existing in rather complete isolation from one another. But there are no hypotheses of the same empirical order which are capable of relating them to one another so that the resulting propositions will serve as methodic controls of the formation of future desires and purposes, and, thereby, of new valuations. The material is ample. But the means for bringing its constituents into such connections that fruit is borne are lacking. This lack of means for bringing actual valuations into relation with one another is partly the cause and partly the effect of belief in standards and ideals of value that lie outside ("above" is the usual term) actual valuations. It is cause in so far as some method of control of desires and purposes is such an important desideratum that in the absence of an empirical method, *any* conception that seems to satisfy the need is grasped at. It is the effect in that a priori theories, once they are formed and have obtained prestige, serve to conceal the necessity for concrete methods of relating valuations and, by so doing, provide intellectual instruments for placing impulses and desires in a context where the very place they occupy affects their evaluation.

However, the difficulties that stand in the way are, in the main, practical. They are supplied by traditions, customs, and institutions which persist without being subjected to a systematic empirical investigation and which constitute the most influential source of further desires and ends. This is supplemented by a priori theories serving, upon the whole, to "rationalize" these desires and ends so as to give them apparent intellectual status and prestige. Hence it is worth while to note that the same obstacles once existed in the subject matters now ruled by scientific methods. Take, as an outstanding example, the difficulties experienced in getting a hearing for the Copernican astronomy a few centuries ago. Traditional and customary beliefs which were sanctioned and maintained by powerful institutions regarded the new scientific ideas as a menace. Nevertheless, the methods which yielded propositions verifiable in terms of actual observations and experimental evidence maintained themselves, widened their range, and gained continually in influence.

The propositions which have resulted and which now form the substantial content of physics, of chemistry, and, to a growing extent, of biology, provide the very means by which the change which is required can be introduced into beliefs and ideas purporting to deal with human and social phenomena. Until natural science had attained to something approaching its present estate, a grounded empirical theory of valuation, capable of serving in turn as a method of regulating the production of new valuations, was out of the question. Desires and interests produce consequences only when the activities in which they are expressed take effect in the environment by interacting with physical conditions. As long as there was no adequate knowledge of physical conditions and no well-grounded propositions regarding their relations to one another (no known "laws"), the kind of forecast of the consequences of alternative desires and purposes involved in their evaluation was impossible. When we note how recently—in comparison with the length of time man has existed on earth—the arts and technologies employed in strictly physical affairs have had scientific support, the backward conditions of the arts connected with the social and political affairs of men provides no ground for surprise.

Psychological science is now in much the same state in which astronomy, physics, and chemistry were when they first emerged as genuinely experimental sciences, yet without such a science systematic theoretical control of valuation is impossible; for without competent psychological knowledge the force of the human factors which interact with environing nonhuman conditions to produce consequences cannot be estimated. This statement is purely truistic, since knowledge of the human conditions *is* psychological science. For over a century, moreover, the ideas central to what passed for psychological knowledge were such as actually obstructed that foresight of consequences which is required to control the formation of ends-in-view. For when psychological subject matter was taken to form a psychical or mentalistic realm set over against the physical environment, inquiry, such as it was, was deflected into the metaphysical problem of the possibility of interaction between the mental and the physical and away from the problem central in evaluation, namely, that of discovering the concrete interactions between human behavior and environing conditions which determine the actual consequences of desires and purposes. A grounded theory of the phenomena of human behavior is as much a prerequisite of a theory of valuation as is a theory of the behavior of physical (in the sense of nonhuman) things. The development of a science of the phenomena of living creatures was an unqualified prerequisite of the development of a sound psychology. Until biology supplied the material facts which lie between the nonhuman and the human, the apparent traits of the latter were so different from those of the former that the doctrine of a complete gulf between the two seemed to be the only plausible one. The missing link in the chain of knowledge that terminates in grounded valuation propositions is the biological. As that link is in process of forging, we may expect the time soon to arrive in which the obstacles to development of an empirical theory of valuation will be those of habits and traditions that flow from institutional and class interests rather than from intellectual deficiencies.

Need for a theory of human relations in terms of a sociology which might perhaps instructively be named cultural anthropology is a further condition of the development of a theory of valuation as an effective instrumentality, for human organisms live in a cultural environment. There is no desire and no interest which, in its distinction from raw impulse and strictly organic appetite, is not what it is because of transformation effected in the latter by their interaction with the cultural environment. When current theories are examined which, quite properly, relate valuation with desires and interests, nothing is more striking than their neglect—so extensive as to be systematic—of the role of cultural conditions and institutions in the shaping of desires and ends and thereby of valuations. This neglect is perhaps the most convincing evidence that can be had of the substitution of dialectical manipulation of the concept of desire for investigation of desires and valuations as concretely existent facts. Furthermore, the notion that an adequate theory of human behavior—including particularly the phenomena of desire and purpose—can be formed by considering individuals apart from the cultural setting in which they live, move, and have their being—a theory which may justly be called metaphysical individualism—has united with the metaphysical belief in a mentalistic realm to keep valuation-phenomena in subjection to unexamined traditions, conventions, and institutionalized customs.[2] The separation alleged to exist between the "world of facts" and the "realm of values" will disappear from human beliefs only as valuation-phenomena are seen to have their immediate source in biological modes of behavior and to owe their concrete content to the influence of cultural conditions.

The hard-and-fast impassible line which is supposed by some to exist between "emotive" and "scientific" language is a reflex of the gap which now exists between the intellectual and

[2] The statement, sometimes made, that metaphysical sentences are "meaningless" usually fails to take account of the fact that culturally speaking they are very far from being devoid of meaning, in the sense of having significant cultural effects. Indeed, they are so far from being meaningless in this respect that there is no short dialectic cut to their elimination, since the latter can be accomplished only by concrete applications of scientific method which modify cultural conditions. The view that sentences having a nonempirical reference are meaningless, is sound in the sense that what they purport or pretend to mean cannot be given intelligibility, and this fact is presumably what is intended by those who hold this view. Interpreted as symptoms or signs of actually existent conditions, they may be and usually are highly significant, and the most effective criticism of them is disclosure of the conditions of which they are evidential.

the emotional in human relations and activities. The split which exists in present social life between ideas and emotions, especially between ideas that have *scientific* warrant and uncontrolled emotions that dominate practice, the split between the affectional and the cognitive, is probably one of the chief sources of the maladjustments and unendurable strains from which the world is suffering. I doubt if an adequate explanation upon the psychological side of the rise of dictatorships can be found which does not take account of the fact that the strain produced by separation of the intellectual and the emotional is so intolerable that human beings are willing to pay almost any price for the semblance of even its temporary annihilation. We are living in a period in which emotional loyalties and attachments are centered on objects that no longer command that intellectual loyalty which has the sanction of the methods which attain valid conclusions in scientific inquiry, while ideas that have their origin in the rationale of inquiry have not as yet succeeded in acquiring the force that only emotional ardor provides. The *practical* problem that has to be faced is the establishment of cultural conditions that will support the kinds of behavior in which emotions and ideas, desires and appraisals, are integrated.

If, then, discussion in the earlier sections of this study seems to have placed chief emphasis upon the importance of valid *ideas* in formation of the desires and interests which are the sources of valuation, and to have centered attention chiefly upon the possibility and the necessity of control of this ideational factor by empirically warranted matters-of-fact, it is because the *empirical* (as distinct from a priori) theory of valuation is currently stated in terms of desire as emotional in isolation from the ideational. In fact and in net outcome, the previous discussion does not point in the least to supersession of the emotive by the intellectual. Its only and complete import is the need for their integration in behavior—behavior in which, according to common speech, the head and the heart work together, in which, to use more technical language, prizing and appraising unite in direction of action. That growth of knowledge of the physical—in the sense of the nonpersonal—has limited the range of freedom of human action in relation to such things as light, heat, electricity, etc., is so absurd in view of what has actually taken place that no one holds it. The operation of desire in producing the valuations that influence human action will also be liberated when they, too, are ordered by verifiable propositions regarding matters-of-fact.

The chief *practical* problem with which the present *Encyclopedia* is concerned, the unification of science, may justly be said to center here, for at the present time the widest gap in knowledge is that which exists between humanistic and non-humanistic subjects. The breach will disappear, the gap be filled, and science be manifest as an operating unity in fact and not merely in idea when the conclusions of impersonal non-humanistic science are employed in guiding the course of distinctively human behavior, that, namely, which is influenced by emotion and desire in the framing of means and ends; for desire, having ends-in-view, and hence involving valuations, is the characteristic that marks off human from nonhuman behavior. On the other side, the science that is put to distinctively human use is that in which warranted ideas about the nonhuman world are integrated with emotion as human traits. In this integration not only is science itself *a* value (since it is the expression and the fulfilment of a special human desire and interest) but it is the supreme means of the valid determination of all valuations in all aspects of human and social life.

Selected Bibliography

AYER, A. J. *Language, Truth and Logic.* New York, 1936.

DEWEY, JOHN. *Essays in Experimental Logic.* Pp. 349–89. Chicago, 1916.

———. *Experience and Nature.* "Lectures upon the Paul Carus Foundation, First Series." 1st ed., Chicago, 1925; 2d ed., New York, 1929.

———. *Human Nature and Conduct.* New York, 1922.

———. *Logical Conditions of a Scientific Treatment of Morality.* Chicago, 1903. Reprinted from *The Decennial Publications of the University of Chicago, First Series,* III, 115–39.

———. *The Quest for Certainty.* New York, 1929.

———. *Art as Experience.* New York, 1934.

DEWEY, JOHN, and TUFTS, J. H. *Ethics.* Rev. ed. New York, 1932.

DEWEY, JOHN, et al. *Creative Intelligence.* New York, 1917.

JOERGENSEN, J. "Imperatives and Logic," *Erkenntnis,* VII (1938), 288–96.

KALLEN, H. "Value and Existence in Philosophy, Art and Religion," in *Creative Intelligence,* ed. JOHN DEWEY et al. New York, 1917.

KÖHLER, W. *Place of Value in a World of Fact.* New York, 1938.

KRAFT, VIKTOR. *Die Grundlagen einer wissenschaftlichen Wertlehre.* Vienna, 1937.

LAIRD, JOHN. *The Idea of Value.* Cambridge, 1929.

MEAD, G. H. "Scientific Method and the Moral Sciences," *International Journal of Ethics,* XXXIII (1923), 229–47.

MOORE, G. E. *Principia ethica.* London, 1903.

NEURATH, OTTO. *Empirische Soziologie; der wissenschaftliche Gehalt der Geschichte und Nationalökonomie.* Vienna, 1931.

PELL, O. A. H. *Value Theory and Criticism.* New York, 1930.

PERRY, RALPH BARTON. *General Theory of Value.* New York, 1926. Also articles in the *International Journal of Ethics* (1931), *Journal of Philosophy* (1931), and *Philosophical Review* (1932).

PRALL, DAVID, W. "A Study in the Theory of Value," *University of California Publications in Philosophy,* III, No. 2 (1918), 179–290.

———. "In Defense of a 'Worthless' Theory of Value," *Journal of Philosophy,* XX (1923), 128–37.

REID, JOHN. *A Theory of Value.* New York, 1938.

RUSSELL, B. *Philosophical Essays.* New York, 1910.

SCHLICK, MORITZ. *Fragen der Ethik.* Vienna, 1930. English trans., *Problems of Ethics.* New York, 1939.

STUART, HENRY WALDGRAVE. "Valuation as Logical Process," in *Studies in Logical Theory,* ed. JOHN DEWEY et al. *The Decennial Publications of the University of Chicago,* Vol. XI. Chicago, 1903.